THE LOST THEATRES OF SHEFFIELD

THE
LOST THEATRES
OF SHEFFIELD

By
Bryen D Hillerby

Wharncliffe Publishing

First Published in 1999 by
Wharncliffe Publishing
an imprint of
Pen and Sword Books Limited,
47 Church Street, Barnsley,
South Yorkshire. S70 2AS

For up-to-date information on other titles produced under the
Wharncliffe imprint, please telephone or write to:

Wharncliffe Publishing
FREEPOST
47 Church Street
Barnsley
South Yorkshire S70 2BR
Telephone (24 hours): 01226 - 734555

ISBN: 1-871647-53-3

A CIP catalogue record of this book is available from the
British Library

Cover illustration: *The Empire,* courtesy of Sheffield City Libraries

Printed in Great Britain by
Redwood Books, Trowbridge, Wiltshire

CONTENTS

*This book is dedicated to my dear friend
Wendy Valentine, recalling the golden days
of pantomime in the 1960s.*

The author with Wendy Valentine, Teignmouth, Devon. 1999

FOREWORD

~

When Bryen asked me to write an introduction to this book, I was naturally delighted to accept. Sheffield has its theatrical roots firmly planted in the Music Hall, of which I have always been a true exponent. I appeared in pantomime with '*Aladdin*', at the *Lyceum* for the 1996 – 1997 season. It is a beautifully restored, intimate theatre. I sincerely hope that the readers of this book will receive as much pleasure from it, as I have been given from fifty years of showbusiness.

Danny La Rue. 1998.

The author with Mr Danny La Rue.

INTRODUCTION

It is a dank, foggy night in the city centre as theatre-goers scurry home in the lamplight via the trams. This could be a typical 1800s scene but not so, since, as I put the finishing touches to this book it is November 1999. The lamps are no longer gas; the bone shakers now Supertrams; but the *Lyceum* theatre still stands as a lasting monument to the glory that was once the theatres of Sheffield. Cobwebbed now by time, but they all had their day in the historical wealth of the world that we call show business.

*'If the theatre is to succeed as a work of art
it must first succeed as a business.'* Sir Henry Irving (1838-1905)

Famous for 'The Bells'. The first British actor to receive a knighthood.

Act I: Overture and Beginners Please

SHEFFIELD AND ITS THEATRICAL ORIGINS IN THE EIGHTEENTH CENTURY

The earliest recorded dramatic performance took place in Sheffield Castle (which was destroyed by order of Parliament in 1648), on 23 April 1581 on the Feast of St George. Mary Stuart, Queen of Scots (1542-1587) was imprisoned there by Earl Shrewsbury (husband of Bess' of the famous Hardwick Hall more window than wall). His men performed this tragedy just six years before her death by execution at Fotheringay Castle, Northamptonshire. Indeed, an auspicious start for the town's theatrical infancy. Over one hundred years after the Royal performance, in 1700, the Pepper Alley Playhouse was established by John Leighton.

The Town Hall was also let in 1727 to a strolling theatre company, by which time the origins of mediaeval Sheffield were at an end. As the town grew, so did the theatrical baby. Nourished by progress, it thrived and soon afterwards the first public playhouse grew up in Angel Court which was actually the yard of the Angel Inn (1728-1762). It was under the direction of Stephen Green and had elegant scenery. It was located in Angel Street, off Nursery Street (this was geographically a few doors from where the infamous villain Charlie Peace was to be born in the early eighteenth century, but more of him later). Although not officially recognised, this playhouse flourished for the next twenty years in smoky old Sheffield, despite Puritanical prejudice. Tickets for shows at the Angel, were also on sale at the George Inn on High Street. At this time, plays were also put on in the yard of another Angel Inn in Button Lane, Moor Head (which at the time was literally out in the countryside). Once a coaching house and hostelry, this inn retained its Georgian appearance for many years and the main entrance was in the courtyard which was approached through an archway.

One of Sheffield's oldest inns, it had in its time been lit by candle; paraffin; gas and electricity. (The oldest *Angel Inn*, in Grantham, dates from 1213). Sheffield's theatrical child had reached maturity in 1761 when a new playhouse was proposed.

During the summer of 1811, Robert Bennett (1788-1819; father of Sir William Sterndale Bennett), became organist of St Paul's Parish Church, Sheffield. (Demolished in 1938). In 1812, he was performing concerts in the theatre and Assembly Rooms. In the passing of time the Theatre and Assembly Rooms had a long and illustrious life as part of the original *Theatre Royal*, whose history is outlined in this book.

Locations of six of the Lost Theatres of Sheffield, circled. Reproduced from the ordinance survey map of 1905.

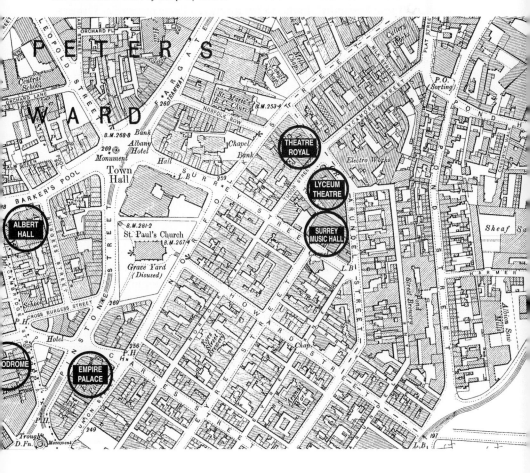

THE UNDERGROUND: SURREY: GAIETY: BRITTANIA: GRAND: SURREY STREET: THE PHOENIX, AND OTHER HALLS

$\sim$

Lets all go to the Music Hall - The nineteenth century West Bar was named after Sheffield's only recorded town gate and known as the 'Little Piccadilly'. In the 1890s this was a lively place on a Saturday night with a profusion of pubs; Music Halls; street entertainers; quack medics and the ever watchful pickpockets and villains. Horse drawn trams took you there but these were unpopular with the general public and caused much conflict with carters and draymen who were off loading! This was an area replete with both grace and flamboyant bawdiness, both essential parts of the city's theatrical history. From pot house to palace, the Music Halls rose from their origins in harmonic rooms adjoining licensed premises to the more important traditional venues. Their financial assets were raised by means of 'wet money', that it to say the sales of beer. Inside, the halls reeked of tobacco and ale and many famous names of the day began their careers in them, the audience being almost exclusively working class. Sheffield was no exception, except for the humour being geared to the Northern taste. The acts were many and varied, with much to offer through an atmosphere which was often smoky, loud and unruly. At the edge of the stage above the orchestra was the chairman's table. He had to be ready to perform at the drop of a hat, because artistes were notoriously unpunctual. One of Sheffield's best chairmen was W B Field whose signature tune was *'Tommy, make room for me'*. Very often the paid performers were joined by the Hall's owners and their families. The 'turns' consisted of naughty comics, magic acts and ribald community singing led by the Master of Ceremonies, 'Mr Chairman'. Animals were often featured; these included a rather unlikely singing pig!, and during one performance a marmoset monkey escaped from the parrot cage in which it was kept and caused mayhem among the audience! The owner was one 'Barrassford' a well known touring continental animal trainer. With regard to the performers,

the point was that they looked like 'artistes', quite different from the clientele and with their own style of dress and make-up. Regular Sheffield stars names read like an ABC of Music Hall.

There were many famous artistes of the day; saucy London cockney Miss Marie Lloyd, real name Matilda Alice Victoria Wood. (1870-1922), 'Queen of the Music Hall', with her shrugs, winks and gestures, quite undeniably a star. Marie shared the same background as her audiences and sang about booze and the bailiffs, a world they knew only too well. '*Don't Dilly Dally*', also known as '*My old Man*', perhaps the archetypal Marie Lloyd song, which dates from the time of the Great War, was performed wearing a battered straw boater, shabby dress and shawl, while carrying a touchingly simple birdcage. She died at the age of only fifty two, her reputation was legendary.

Vesta Victoria, (1874-1951), also sang suggestive songs and immortalised '*Daddy Wouldn't Buy Me a Bow Wow*'. Miss Gertie Gitana was the star who never failed to shine, her real name was Gertrude Mary Astbury (1887-1957), she was a popular pantomine artiste who married Don Ross. Her great

OurMarie' Lloyd 'Queen of the Music Halls' (1870-1922)

claim to fame is that she popularised the song 'Nelly Dean'.

Little Tich, whose real name was Harry Relph (1867-1928), (big boot dancer) and Dan Leno, the world champion clog dancer, also played the Sheffield Halls. In his later years Dan Leno won further fame as perhaps the greatest of all pantomime dames. During these naughty eighteen nineties, the women were the 'Kings of Drag'. Famous male impersonators

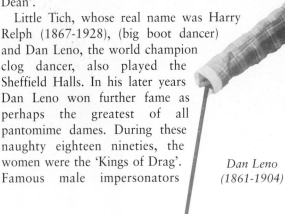

Dan Leno (1861-1904)

included; Miss Vesta Tilley, real name Matilda Alice Powles, (1864-1952), the 'Idol of the Halls'; Miss Bessie Bonehill and Miss Ella Shields (1879-1952), and Miss Hetty King (1883-1972), who wore nautical attire to sing '*All the Nice Girls Love a Sailor*' and '*Piccadilly*'. Songs 'en travesti' were always a popular part of Music Hall. On the other side of the coin, equally famous female impersonators were Scott Barrie - a favourite Northern 'Dame' comedian, Mr Malcolm Scott (1872-1929), 'The woman who knows' who played Nell Gwynn and 'The Dictoire Girl!' Barbette, real name Van Der Clyde, born 1899, put on a beautiful and daring low wire and trapeze act. She appeared in a flowing silver lace and rich lame train, with elaborate wig of silver and gold, topped with a plume of feathers. Her eyes were shaded a lurid green! Slowly undressing to just jewels on her breasts and stomach she performed daring acrobatic feats. Jumping down from the wire, she took her bows and tore off the wig, to reveal in fact the bald and bony head of a young man of athletic build, far from lacking in muscle. The audience was aghast at this dramatic revelation!

From America came what was perhaps one of the first American acts to cross the Atlantic, Mr Julian Eltinge, a celebrated female impersonator.

Other famous acts of the day were, the beautiful Miss Happy Fanny Fields, another American and Go.won.go Mohawk, who signed all her photographs, 'Aboriginally Yours' and not forgetting Miss Mona Vivian, the celebrated singer. A buxom Miss Florrie Ford, real name Flanagan, (1876-1940), sang '*Down at the old Bull and Bush*' which became her signature tune on the Halls. She also popularised the Jack Judge song '*Tipperary*' and was the female epitome of Music Hall gusto, from ample bosom to plump thighs. This celebrated chorus singer was in fact Australian!

However, the entertainment was not always

Miss Vesta Tilley,
Idol of the halls.
(1864-1952)

Mr Malcolm Scott. 'The
woman who knows'.

Miss Mona Vivian   *Go.won.go Mohawk, 'aboriginally yours'.*

drag and comic singers. Speciality acrobatic acts were often presented; the original '*Daring Young Man on the Flying Trapeze*', the title of a song written by George Leybourne, was a Frenchman whose name 'Leotard' is still associated with the style of tights he wore. Leotard performed without a safety net. He died of smallpox while in France, he was only 28 years old.

Legends of the Music Hall included Miss Jenny Hill 'The Vital Spark' (1850-1896). She had a repertoire of some thirty songs, the best remembered of all being the beautiful '*The Boy I Love is Up in the Gallery*', she was paid the highest salary of any artist of her day.

One of the more voluptuous singers of the day was; Miss Harriett Vernon. Miss Lottie Collins, (1869-1910), made '*Ta Ra Ra Boom De Ay*' famous during the 1890s and the dance craze it inspired. Lottie was the mother of Miss Jose Collins, who became famous as the 'Maid of The Mountains'.

Many of the artistes who appeared in Sheffield theatres in the early days of their careers included, Miss Nellie Wallace, (1870-1948), who played the Halls of Sheffield, as did Miss Bessie Belwood, real name Elizabeth Anne Katherine Mahoney,

Miss Happy Fanny Fields, popular American singer (1881-1961).

(1857-1896). She was a strikingly handsome and wild woman and singer of Cockney songs like, '*What Cheer Ria*'.

'Coram', (Thomas Whitaker. 1883-1937), the Sheffield born ventriloquist, with his dummy 'Jerry', made his fortune on the London stage. He was the father of Billy Whitaker, (1914-1995) comedian, who worked with Mimi Law. Mr Fred Barnes, (1884-1938), became a big star, being a polished, immaculately dressed artiste with a good light baritone voice, who made songs like '*Give Me the Moonlight, Give Me the Girl*' famous. He also performed the original version of '*On Mother Kelly's Doorstep*' (later performed by Randolph Sutton 1889-1969). This song has been performed in recent years by Mr Danny La Rue. Barnes pursued an eccentric lifestyle, among other things he consorted openly with men, very unwise in those days!, which inevitably resulted in a scandal. His career fell into a severe decline, and he passed out of the limelight during the 1930s.

Perhaps the most moving singer of all in her day, was Miss Ella Shields, from America, singing '*I'm Burlington Bertie from Bow*', in the attire of a tramp fallen on hard times. Written by her husband William Hargreaves, it was a parody on the life of the Prince of Wales. One verse ended ...'*I had a banana with Lady Diana, I'm Burlington...*', (Lady

Miss Florrie Forde, famous principal boy. (1876-1940)   *Miss Harriet Vernon, buxom music hall star.*

Diana was Lady Diana Manners). What greater honour was there than to be immortalised in the words of the most famous of all Music Hall songs?

Among other performers around this time who have left an indelible memory in the songs they made famous are; Mr Charles Coburn (1852-1945), '*The Man Who Broke the Bank at Monte Carlo*', Mr Albert Chevalier, real name Colin McCallum (1861-1923), '*My Old Dutch*', Mr Eugene Stratton, '*Lily of Laguna*', Mr Gus Elen, (1862-1940), sang the sardonic '*Houses Inbetween*'. They are still remembered with affection today, as is Mr Harry Champion with '*Boiled Beef and Carrots*' and Mr Billy Merson with '*The Spaniard that Blighted My Life*'.

South Yorkshire was also the scene of a remarkable bit of Music Hall history, when the great high wire artiste 'Charles Blondin' (real name Jean Francois Gravelet), presented his act in Rotherham in 1895, at the age of 71. World famous for his crossing of Niagara Falls on a high wire stunt, he came out of retirement to put on this final performance. Audiences at first refused to believe that he was the original performer, but indeed he was! Most of the great Music Hall artistes trod the boards as soon as they could walk and frequently died whilst still working. The pace of life and work for performers was tough and often quite literally, killing. Mr Mark Sheridan, whose catchphrase was '*Here we are again*', shot himself after being booed on stage. George Formby senior, real name James Booth (1880-1921), whose catchphrase was, '*Coughing better tonight*', utilised his uncontrollable cough in his act when he was in fact dying, while the great Dan Leo (George Galvin), eventually went mad on stage in 1901 and finally died in 1904 at the age of 43.

Billy Merson

These events were prominent in the late 1800s and early 1900s, by the mid 1930s, great and irreversible changes were afoot.

The era of the cinema had arrived and when 'Talking Pictures' followed, they eventually resulted in the Music Halls passing into entertainment history. Nowadays, their tradition only survives with the 'City Varieties' Music Hall in Leeds and the dazzling 'road show' tours by such artistes as Mr Danny La Rue, one of the few remaining true exponents of Music Hall. But in the story that follows, we revisit the 'Good Old Days' of the Sheffield Music Hall!

THE UNDERGROUND THEATRE

There is evidence confirming the existence of an 'Underground Music Hall' in the Wicker area of Sheffield in the late 1800s. Miss Edith Glynne, who appeared at The Grand Theatre, Leeds, in the Wilson Barret pantomime '*The Pretty Princess and The Old Man of the Sea*', was paid £2 weekly in 1886 for this prestigious engagement! Prior to this in 1882, she was employed by Mr Thomas Machin, being engaged as a serio to appear at the 'Underground Music Hall', Sheffield. On this occasion her salary was £7-5s to appear for one week only! Obviously only the very best was good enough for the Sheffield audiences in this prestigious Hall.

Footnote: Whether or not it was indeed subterranean has not been ascertained at the time of writing, despite extensive investigation. Neither has the exact location been determined. An appeal for information made by the author over Yorkshire Television in 1998 failed to bring forth any further information.

THE SURREY

Located at 84/6 West Bar, on the junction of West Bar and Workhouse Lane. This was not the original *Surrey Music Hall* but a tavern known as the *Surrey Hotel*. Frank Howson became licensee in June 1907.

Animated pictures were introduced in 1909, following the Hall being renovated and re-decorated, making it an excellent establishment for good variety turns and company pictures. The premises were licensed under the *1909 Cinematograph Act* though the management were taken to task for not employing a fireman! This was the last of the Sheffield Halls to feature old time entertainment with a chairman. The policy of presenting cine-variety continued until 1911. During March 1910 admission profits were still supplemented with the sale of alcohol but, when the film license expired at the end of 1912, Mr Howson agreed not to apply for a renewal. The Hall continued to present live entertainment until he left in 1916. In later years the premises were demolished.

THE GAIETY

Located at 100 West Bar, diagonally opposite the '*London Apprentice*'. Close to the West Bar pump, a water supply known as the '*Work House Well*', on West Bar Green, its stage and dressing rooms were entered from the corner of Corporation Street and Steelhouse Lane. Like most of the Halls in this area it began life as a public house. It was owned by Louis Metzler, a German who also owned a pork butcher's shop adjoining the theatre which he ran as a sideline. The theatre occupied an odd wedge-shaped building and was the most prominent of all the Halls. Admission was 3d, returnable in beer. It boasted smoke rooms; bar parlours and private snugs, (for dubious disorderly entertainments with versatile dancing girls!). The auditorium had a proscenium arch, ornately moulded ceiling and a bar from where patrons could view the onstage acts. Mr Metzler maintained a select house, with slogans outside proclaiming.

'Good clean entertainment guaranteed here, bring your wife and family, enjoy elegance, safety, comfort and respectability'.

George Leybourne, real name Joseph Saunders (1842-1884)), the original singer of '*Champagne Charlie*' appeared here, being paid £3 for the week, a substantial salary for those days. The first 'Lion Comique' he drove up to the theatre in a coach and four! The lightning service

The Gaiety Theatre-100 West Bar.

The Gaiety Theatre, side elevation-Corporation Street.

necessitated retention of a part full glass, otherwise the waiters whisked 'almost finished' glasses away while the patrons watched the show! The Hall was famous for 'Lucy' a tame singing' pig, which wandered freely among the customers. Known to have a liking for the 'old and mild' beer, the customers plied the poor pig with it until it was hopelessly inebriated!

Site of the Gaiety, which was demolished in 1996, despite opposition.

This 'musical' pig, with a chorus of oinks and squeaks created its own mythology. Someone once remarked backstage, '*The theatre was hardly big enough to swing a pig*'!

In 1896, the *Gaiety* faced stiff competition from the newly opened *Empire Theatre* and in addition, changing licensing laws forced closure. The building survived several vicissitudes over the years that followed. The company of Ellis Pearson and Son Ltd used the premises as a glass warehouse in the 1970s and in 1987 it was partly occupied by Ellis, Son and Paramore (a surgical appliance maker, famous for trusses!). Local historian, Eric Wilcox enthused over the original arched external bar entrance and preserved foyer site. When alterations were made to the premises they were carefully preserved behind boardings for historical interest. The original staircase and sloping auditorium floor survived intact. There was even a pillar of fluted design which had remnants of the original gold leaf atop! The building survived boarded up until 1996, when demolition swept away the preserved features despite much opposition at the time. A local business resident informed me that a quantity of theatre bill posters were also discovered but destroyed by fire without any concern for their historical interest.

THE BRITANNIA

Located at 121 West Bar adjoining the old fire station, capacity: 1,000 – this was one of the oldest Music Halls in the country, dating back to before 1860. It backed on to the old *Tankard Inn* owned by one John Richdale. Originally the pub was on the ground floor and the hall above. Run by the Richdale family, who often appeared on stage in addition to guest artistes, for the entertainment of the patrons. A 'posh hall', like the *Gaiety*, the admission charge was 6d, (2.5p), including a pint of beer thrown in, or over you! Mr Louis Metzler controlled the *Britannia*. He also owned the *Gaiety* and the neighbouring 'London Apprentice'. The three theatres were actually public houses with a stage erected inside them. The famous clog dancer Dan Leno appeared here as a child and was seen by Charles Dickens who said, '*Good little man, you'll make headway*'. (Dan Leno's 'double shuffle' is still the basis for tap routines worldwide. In the latter part of his career, he became the most famous of pantomime dames at London's *Drury Lane Theatre*). Outside the *Britannia* a prominent sign always stated '*No shawls*'. Admission was 3d and the ticket was in the form of a brass token stamped, '*Britannia Music Hall*' around the rim and 'Old Tankard Inn' on the face. The reverse stated admission 3d, returned in refreshment 2d. so patrons could surrender the entry 'coin' and receive a pint of beer from the bar worth 2d! Often a full house numbering a thousand, sat with drinks at tables and often showed disapproval of the artistes performance by hurling halfpennies at them with the intent of cutting their faces! This Hall was typical of its kind, riotously rough and sordidly unwholesome. This type of Music Hall started to die out when strict licensing law changes and the introduction of basic fire regulations caused the Britannia to close in 1895. The building had several changes of purpose, once being altered and used as a warehouse by William Greene and Co stove grate manufacturers and home improvement specialists. During these alterations, the internal and external measurements of the building were compared. A marked difference was noted and on investigation a false wall was discovered at the rear of the

The Britannia Theatre located at 121 West Bar. This was one of the oldest Music Halls in the country and dated back to before 1860. This photograph was taken in the 1970s.

This 1999 photograph, shows the garage forecourt which now occupies the space where The Britannia Theatre once stood.

building behind which was found the original stage area, which was identified by historian Andrew Woodfield. When the area was cleared, a proscenium arch measuring nineteen feet wide, fourteen feet high was fully visible, with a stage forty feet wide and complete back cloth rollers. Bars supporting a trapeze and its climbing ladder were also still intact. On 26 July 1978 the official receiver held an auction, selling off what remained of the fixtures and fittings. In 1987 the building was occupied by Harmony Wedding World (proprietor Mrs Joan Spalding) who stated that the neglect was tragic. Banister rails had been stolen, modern walls dissected the auditorium and rain leaked in through rotting windows. The circle and gallery tiers were still just evident. Nobody cared and the rotting building was later badly damaged by fire and subsequently demolished.

THE GRAND THEATRE

Located on West Bar tram junction, at the corner of Spring Street and Coulson Street and facing up Snig Hill (behind *The Old Packhorse Inn*). The architect in 1893 was Mr W.H. Lancashire. Sadly, the original builders and subsequent improvers cannot be traced. The theatre was built in the late 1860s and was originally called the *West Bar Hall*. Like the *Gaiety* along the road, admission was 3d, returnable in beer. Patrons were served at tables in the gallery or on the ground floor, whilst watching the local talents perform. Basically a public house, later renamed '*The Bijou*', it boasted a large auditorium and stage. It was renamed '*Squints Theatre*' under the ownership of Mr Alfred Milner who had a serious squint. He reputedly owned a marvellous oil painting collection.

The theatre was renovated and reopened on 18 December 1874 as '*The New Star Music Hall*'. It was so named for having a star shaped, flaring gas jet over the entrance doors. During this period, the theatre had a regular infamous patron, the later notorious Charlie Peace-king of

The Grand Theatre-West Bar, facing Snig Hill. Photographed in 1930 when it was a public house.

the burglars. He was often seen there with a Mrs Dyson whose husband he murdered at Banner Cross in 1876. (He was hanged for this murder in York during 1879). A dingy appearance prevailed over the exterior due to playbills being plastered on the windows and walls. Inside, it was a well appointed hall with tasteful furnishings but a low class clientele. However, it prospered and was again remodelled, reopening on 26 December 1887 as '*The Grand Theatre*' under the new ownership of Mr Alexander Stacey. Though practically rebuilt, the hall was extensively altered again under the ownership of Edward and Oxford Welding, two brothers from Aberdeen. It reopened on 27 March 1893 with a new plastered frontage which, despite the efforts of designers and plasterers alike, remained undistinguished. The auditorium was charmingly laid out with stalls seats of red plush. Likewise the central balcony seats, which were also divided from the sides and promenades by a permanent screen. Downstairs, the rear pit seating was spartan, with matting or oilcloth floor coverings. At each level were two private boxes and an ornamental ceiling bearing the names of famous composers flanked by the goddess Venus with cupids. Pit and stalls entrances were in West Bar; while the balcony entrance was in Coulson Street. Each part of the house had an imposing lounge with large bar and an indicator to inform patrons of the current act on stage. Lighting was entirely by electricity throughout creating a cosy atmosphere. Many headliners played there including Mr Charles Coburn. Since the Weldings found the Hall uneconomic to run and their rebuilding plans had been met with disapproval from the licensing authority, it closed again on 1 January 1895.

From 7 October of that year it was opened again, unsuccessfully, by Mr H.J. Johnston. Mr Francis William MacNaghten, an influential entrepreneur reopened the hall, introducing twice nightly variety performances in order to fight off the competition from the recently opened *Empire Theatre*. This policy was a great success and with further renovation the Hall, though being small, reopened on 1 August 1896 as '*The Grand Theatre of Varieties*'. Despite the stiff competition from the star names at the *Empire* (opened 1895), the Hall maintained a regular audience who enjoyed acts of high calibre. Reduced admission prices were, Pit 2d; Stalls 4d; Balcony 6d; Centre Balcony stalls 9d. Private boxes; two shillings per chair. Externally *The Grand* resembled a pub more than a theatre, refreshments being offered at public house prices in an extensive advertising campaign. *The Grand*'s potential was however limited. Though primarily a variety theatre, it occasionally featured dramatic sketches and with a mounting frequency, animated pictures. Still a novelty, in November 1896, they were short but billed as a major attraction for example Lumieres 'cinematographe' was demonstrated at *The Grand*. During February 1910, renovative decoration was carried out, including the construction of a fire-proof box to satisfy the Cinematographe act of that year. Films were made of highly inflammable cellulose nitrate, a fire hazard bordering on the explosive! After a succession of managers, Mr Arthur William Turpin was appointed in July 1907, remaining until the closing weeks of 1908. New owners were John Smiths (Tadcaster) and the MacNaghten Vaudeville syndicate, who had become sole lessees in March 1907. *The Grand* was primarily described as a cinema at this time. On opening night, an acrobat, Naomi Etharoo, who did contortions atop a pyramid of glass bottles!, appeared with Fred Newby, popular comedian. From 5 October 1908, the presentation was '*The Adventures of Nick Carter*' with the supporting film and variety acts. By November 1910 the lessee was Elisha Charles Clayton, a film renter who in later years became a leading cinema proprietor. In October 1912, the manager was J.C. Morgan, while in June 1914, it was Sydney Walford Grout. During the summer of 1914, further restoration was done and a new kalee projector installed. The three bars were also divided from the main auditorium at this time. Admission prices of 1d; 2d and 3d were low and were not increased even at this time. The Hall remained open throughout the First World War. In 1917, Mr T. Ryan was manager and the cinema was sold by auction on 27 January 1920 to 'Grand Picture Houses Sheffield'. They proposed building a 'Superkinema' on the site and the cinema closed down in November or December 1920. The company bought adjoining cottages but the housing shortage deterred evictions for demolition. The Sheffield cinema trade was also undergoing a massive slump in the early post war years and the construction of a 2,500 capacity cinema was a less than attractive proposition. *The Grand*'s rear wall partially collapsed in January 1921 following which renovations were carried out but the local authority opposed the reopening for use as a cinema or Music Hall. In November of that year, a public investment prospectus was issued with the aim of raising the £85,000 required to build the new cinema. Support was only modest, since people were now moving away from the West Bar area. The Hall reopened on 8 December 1922 as a trade show centre for the Sheffield branch of the Cinematograph Exhibitors Association, but no public film exhibition license was granted. Trade shows for various cinemas were held with decreasing frequency and ceased on 15 June 1924. Although the 'Superkinema' plan was reconsidered, it was never a realistic scheme. *The Grand* was used as a shelter for the homeless and food kitchen, eventually becoming derelict. The new building plan was finally abandoned in 1938, when the building was sold to the local authority for a road widening scheme and demolished in August of that year.

THE SURREY STREET MUSIC HALL

Located at 79 Surrey Street. The Hall was built in 1823 and opened with an inaugural speech by Dr Younge, the well respected town improver, in 1824. The architects were J.G. Weightman and M.E. Hadfield. This was a deceptively large building, one room alone being capable of holding 1,000 people. The interior walls were decorated with medallion portraits of eminent composers. A wagon roof, hollow walls and large rooms beneath created highly praised acoustics. It was regarded as being more highbrow than other Sheffield theatres, presenting concerts of classical music and poetry readings! Founded by the Yorkshire Choral Concert Society, the Hall presented regular recitals by great artists of high calibre, including; Moscheles; Paganini and Miss Jenny Lind, 'The Swedish Nightingale'. A plain woman, she claimed that her voice was a gift from God, which radiated her beauty from within. For a short time only, the original and celebrated General Tom Thumb, world renowned American gentleman in miniature appeared here. The tiniest man alive was presented to Queen Victoria on 2 November 1857, under the patronage of the principal Crown heads of Europe. In approximately 1836, a series of lectures took place and included a public debate between Alfred Bywater and Richard Otley on 'Materiality and

The Music Hall-Surrey Street, built in 1823. Its largest rooms accommodated 1000 patrons.

Immortality of the Soul'! In December 1836 the 'Peristrephic' presented a moving panorama of the city of Jerusalem-the venerable city of holy writing. The presentation included views of the Mount of Olives and Mount Zion. From 1849, an experimental series of promenada concerts were produced entitled, '*For the Million*'.

Charles Dickens attended the Music Hall on several occasions. On Sunday 29 August 1852, when as both manager of the Hall and a remarkable actor, he appeared with friends, one of them being Wilkie Collins, in a play by Bulwer Lytton entitled '*Not so Bad as We Seem*'. A farce was also performed entitled '*Mr Nightingale's Diary*', being jointly written by Dickens and Mark Lemon, the then editor of *Punch*. Dickens played a deaf sexton and a respectable female! This occasion was a huge celebrity-social event for which a special stage was erected. Admission prices were extremely high for the times, being 10s 6d for the Saloon and 7s 6d for the Gallery, because funds were being raised for the '*Guild of Literature and Arts*'. Over 600 people were present and a special train ran from Rotherham. Specially designed souvenir tickets were printed for the occasion. All reports indicate that the event was a roaring success. Dickens appeared previously here in 1848 to read his Mrs Gamp and a

The photograph (right) shows the original public library which was previously The Music Hall-Surrey Street.

The same site (below) photographed in 1999, which is now the Central Library and Graves Art Gallery.

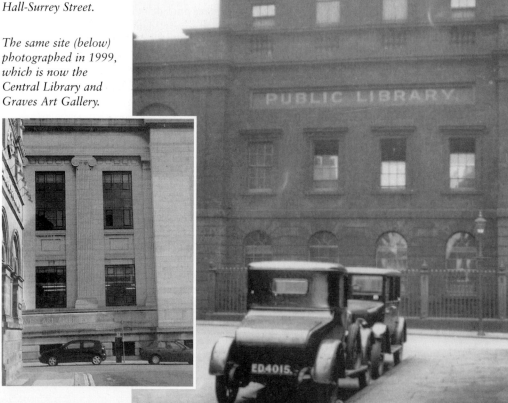

carefully condensed '*The Story of Little Dombey*', (later published as *Dombey and Son*). During the reading he made effective use of a paper-knife to emphasise his points. Seat prices once again were very high; 7s 6d; 5s; 3s and 2s. At a later appearance in 1855, on a Saturday night before Christmas, he read his now celebrated '*A Christmas Carol*'. After the performance, the Lord Mayor, Alderman W. Fawcett presented Mr Dickens with a service of table cutlery, a pair of razors and a pair of fish carvers. This manifestation of gratitude was to thank Mr Dickens for his kindness in returning once more to Sheffield.

The Literary and Philosophical Society (formed in 1822 at the Cutlers Hall) had a team of lecturers who travelled country wide, presenting lectures on a wide variety of topics, appealing to the more serious minded patron. The 'Lit and Phil', as they were colloquially known, rented ground floor rooms in the Hall for over forty years, their lectures being in sharp contrast to the serious music and concerts presented in the Music Hall.

A glorious moment came in 1863, when a group of young men were addressed by T.D. Gregg, delivering a lecture entitled '*The Steam Locomotive as Revealed in the Bible*'! A church conference of clergy and laity was also held there in 1869.

The well-to-do and professional classes promoted many subscription concerts and the Music Hall continued up to the early 1870s with artistes such as Sir William Sterndale Bennett, who made his first public appearance, here in his native town. The poet James Montgomery gave regular readings of his own works and the Hall was also honoured with visits by the distinguished W.M. Thackery. In 1873 the Hall proprietors decided that it was too small for Sheffield's increased demand for more elaborate musical events. This lead to plans being drawn up for a larger hall, resulting in the planning and building of the Albert Hall. However *The Surrey* remained the chief concert and exhibition hall in the city until 1902. It was later in use as a drapery, tailoring and carpets warehouse for Messrs J.G. Graves. This was a mail order company. A substantial customer of the GPO, Mr Graves was frequently at cross purposes with them. *The Surrey* backed on to the *Lyceum*, being situated at the far end of Surrey Street, a short space away from the old Mechanics Institute, where the City Library was founded in 1856 (the space in between the two buildings had many years previously been occupied by a timber merchant). During the First World War the Music Hall was also used as an army recruiting office. Both buildings were demolished in the mid 1930s, being purchased by the corporation to make way for the new Central Library which opened in 1934. The Library building also houses the Graves Art Gallery. Today, on a Friday night the disco lights from

The Surrey public house opposite, play on the exact spot where spectacular Music Hall presentations once took place.

There was of course a warren of lesser known Halls, Sheffield boasting well over a dozen, more than any other town outside London. These included:

The London Apprentice, located at the corner of West Bar and West Bar Green (adjoining Queen Street and opposite the new law courts). The management of the *London Apprentice* refused to admit men in mufflers or caps and women wearing headscarves, or who were unescorted!

The Royal Pavilion, which was located in Norfolk Street. Opening in 1860, with a capacity of 500 to 600 this Hall was regarded as having a most unsavoury reputation. Regardless of this, it was very popular on Friday nights when legs of mutton were given away to lucky raffle prize winners. On the same bill they once advertised *Hamlet* and a farce entitled '*My Wife's Second Floor*'. Adjoining the old *Theatre Royal*, after a short life, during which it was regarded as Sheffield's leading Music Hall, it was partly demolished in 1875, but a section was retained to create refreshment bars for the *Theatre Royal*. The site was built on by John Round Ltd. cutlers whose Tudor showroom and fork works belonged to a pharmacy company. The building was demolished in later years and the site is now an elongated egg-shaped raised grassed area with attractive paving in front of the *Lyceum Theatre*.

Walter Cooper's *Alhambra Music Hall* was located on the corner of Union Street and Charles Street, on an upper floor, above some shops. Built on the site of Lord George Sangers Circus, it burnt down in 1881 and became the site of the later *Empire Theatre*. Mr George (Champagne Charlie) Leybourne sang his most popular song sheet renditions in this Hall.

The Blue Boar, was located on Snig Hill. It was later used as a warehouse by Turners News Ltd.

The Phoenix, Langsett Road and *Heeley Green*, Gleadless Road; both used by very small touring companies and much supported by Sheffield patrons.

The list goes on with, *Ryan's Theatre*, *Durvali's Pavilion* and *The Little Regent Theatre*, Upwell Street, in Grimethorpe.

The *Fleur de Lys* stood on the site of the former Cockayne's store, (now the Argos Superstore). This was a very select house, where Sheffield born Miss Florrie Gallimore sang.

In Barker's Pool was a small but good Hall called *The Union*.

Finally, not forgetting the one that got away! *The Tivoli Music Hall*, located on Burton Street, at the junction of Bilston Street (Penistone Road side). This unhappy story relates to a Music Hall that almost never was. The proprietor, Joseph Crofts Brothwell opened for two days only, there being just two Bank Holiday performances on 5 and 6 of August

1907. Conversion of the premises formerly connected with the production of mineral water, commenced in June 1906 at a cost of £500. The local board of Justices opposed four music and dancing license applications placed for the *Tivoli*. On inspecting the Hall one morning, whilst it was empty, they found the atmosphere intolerable due to the exceptionally high room temperatures, despite the absence of any form of heating! By 15 August the Hall's fate was sealed, the Justices forming the opinion that the entirely unsuitable building could not be structurally altered to make it acceptable to them. Undoubtedly, Music Halls were thought to be disreputable entertainments and in addition it was considered that the *Tivoli*'s location, close to Hillsborough Barracks, may have a disruptive influence on the soldiery, caused by the undesirables attending the performances (which just goes to show that even though the show must go on, your can't win them all!)

THE PHOENIX THEATRE

Located in Langsett Road, directly opposite Hillsborough Barracks. Built by J B Mitchell-Winters and opened on Monday 27 March 1911. Capacity-640.

This theatre presented refined entertainment in the form of both variety turns and films. It had a respectably sized stage. The interior decor was green walls with an ivory ceiling and plasterwork executed in several shades, not dissimilar to that in *The Regent*, Barker's Pool. Miss Irene Card recalled to the author, working in the pay box before her *Empire Theatre* days. *The Phoenix* was wired for the new and highly sophisticated for the day, Western Electric Sound System. Externally, it was built in red brick with a stucco façade above. The frontage was flat with ornamental arches at either side above the exit doors. The central entrance door was reached by a flight of steps and the *Phoenix Theatre* sign was above the entrance. The stage door was to the rear of the left elevation, with its own arch above and the building had a long rectangular roof.

The final presentation was *The Trials of Oscar Wilde*.

The theatre was demolished and the site cleared for the erection of a petrol station.

THE SURREY THEATRE

Located on West Bar, almost opposite the *London Apprentice*. In 1834, Thomas Youdan aged eighteen, came to this area of Sheffield from Ireland as a labourer and was working in nearby Doncaster. In those days, West Bar was a dingy, overcrowded tenement area. A colourful character, he became the landlord of *The Spinks Nest Inn* in 1851. Youdan worked hard and built up his capital and eventually purchased the nearby *Casino* public house and dancing room, a small unpretentious structure. Later acquiring the *Surrey Theatre*, he extended it to incorporate the *Casino* renaming and opening the joined properties as, *Youdans Royal Casino* in 1858. There were entrances in both West Bar and Workhouse Lane. The front of the building was still occupied with small tenements. Free musical entertainments, including sacred music on Sundays with an efficient band, drew the crowds and he prospered in the same year. The building was greatly enlarged to the proportions of a comfortable theatre with museum and picture gallery and renamed *The Surrey Theatre*. Operatic programmes and melodramas were now presented including 'Sweeney Todd - the Demon Barber' and 'Maria Marten - the Murder in the Red Barn', playing to enthusiastic audiences. In 1863, the West Bar tenements were also demolished and the theatre closed for a while and Youdan spent some £30,000 on sensational improvements intending that *The Surrey* would become one of the country's finest entertainment centres. Reputedly it had become the finest theatre outside London, second only to *Covent Garden* and was also the largest public building in Sheffield. The frontage on West Bar had an imposing ante-room adorned by many fine mirrors equal in size to those on the grand staircase at Stafford House, previously thought to be the finest in England. The picture gallery was illuminated by several impressive chandeliers, as was the luxurious smoke room situated above the West Bar entrance. The enlarged theatre now accommodated 1,500 people on rows of wooden seats in the pit, with tier upon tier of boxes draped with light curtaining. At strategic places in the auditorium there were countless gas jets alight for the gentlemen to ignite their cigars and pipes. (Cigarettes were not a popular alternative at this time). These fine jets were modelled on the effigy of Mr Punch, a character from the *Harlequinade*. The stage was equipped to present very ambitious productions.

To the rear in Spring Street, patrons entered the extended underground museum, which was unequalled outside of London. This contained an exhibition of impressive model cities; Indian and Chinese weapons; marble statues; marble busts of the famous; mechanical figures; rare stuffed birds and fine pictures. There was even a menagerie of assorted fine live animals from Wingerworth Hall attached to the Theatre. In addition there was a large buffet and waxworks which featured a notable grouping entitled '*The Judgement of Solomon*'. The ground floor had a saloon containing concert and dining rooms whilst on a floor above the theatre, was a magnificent ballroom. This was decorated with gorgeous mirrors, several fine oil paintings and a magnificent cut-glass chandelier. Obviously, no expense was spared, but one cannot help wondering if this well appointed building was, to say the least, something of a fire hazard?

Externally, the building was very grand, sporting an imposing, great tower which became a local landmark. Stretching over the roof below it was an immense wooden platform for the partaking of dancing during the balmy summer evenings. The platform also incorporated a dining hall. Youdan was by now the undisputed King of the Music Halls, specialising in lurid melodrama, until he over-reached himself completely!

In March 1865, yet another realistic modern drama was staged, Boucicault's '*The Streets of London*', which featured the Great Fire of 1666. Admission prices were: Private boxes, 2s; Amphitheatre, 1s; Boxes, 6d; Gallery, 3d.

On 25 March the play had run for two weeks to the delight of packed houses. Special effects included a grand house fire as the climax of the play. Tarpaulin and wood were ignited and the blaze tackled by real firemen specially recruited by Mr Youdan. The stage fire was lit and the house façade crashed blazing onto the stage with great dramatic effect. The Friday evening performance being over, the gaslights were extinguished at midnight, however it was surmised that some part of the woodwork, probably the flies had been ignited during the performance. At about 2.30am a policeman discovered the building on fire. A ferocious blaze took hold of the theatre which was immediately evacuated by the few remaining employees. In less than five minutes, the flames burst through the roof at the rear of the building and in no time, the whole structure was a roaring mass of fire and smoke. The firemen acted in desperate haste, because explosives, stored in the building and

The Surrey Theatre-West Bar, ablaze, 25 March 1865.

intended to blow off the roof of the stage house had ignited and enhanced the already awful conflagration. At the height of the blaze, fire brigades from several neighbouring towns were in attendance. The fire spread rapidly, threatening to destroy the surrounding West Bar houses, Spring Street and Hick's Lane also being in great danger. The building burned down in such grand style due to its being built largely of wood. The epic fire raged all through the night and until 10.00am the next morning and was not completely extinguished for five days. The building was totally gutted, nothing remaining but the charred walls. Although there was no loss of life, members of the company lost all their own costumes and props. The Mayor, Alderman Thomas Jessop, set up a subscription fund to replace the lost possessions and compensate the

The Surrey Theatre-West Bar proprietor Thomas Youdan (seated foreground) and stage company outside the building shell, the morning after the fire.

company for the loss of their employment. Mr Youdan was totally overwhelmed by this catastrophe and cried like a child. He faced bankruptcy since, against the estimated rebuilding costs of £30,000, there was insurance cover of only £13,000. However, undeterred he began immediate negotiations to purchase *The Adelphi Circus*, a former storeroom in Blonk Street.

Until 1880 *The Surrey Theatre* remained as it had been left by the fire, until *The Sheffield Guardians* purchased the site. In 1881, the Union and Vestry Offices were constructed on the site in the Italian Renaissance style. These were destroyed by enemy action in 1940 and no permanent building replaced them for many years, although a motor showroom was established on the site in 1974.

A somewhat chequered career for the ground where many thousands of people once found pleasure and recreation.

Today the new Law Courts stands on the site!

THE ADELPHI CIRCUS THEATRE

Located on Blonk Street, opposite the cattle market. *The Adelphi* was built in 1837, by Mr Egan. It was reputedly a faithful copy of Astley's famous amphitheatre in Westminster Bridge Road, London. Originally known as *The Circus*, it came under the management of the magnificent Ducrow.

When first built it had a 42ft diameter ring which transformed into a large pit for equestrian acts. This idea being copied from *The Adelphi Theatre*, London. There was also rear stabling capable of accommodating

The Adelphi Circus Theatre, was renamed the Alexandre Theatre in 1865 as shown below. Photographed in 1910.

Alexandre Theatre, at the junction of Blonk Street and Exchange Street.

fourteen horses. Claiming to be the only Sheffield stage capable of accommodating elephants, this was proved in the 1856 pantomime *Bluebeard* (or *Female Curiosity*). An early performance also featured a man putting a freshly blooded hand into a lion's mouth!

In 1865 the theatre was purchased by Thomas Youden and converted into the *Alexandre Music Hall*.

The Blonk Street frontage was an imposing structure, with a handsome Greco-Ionic column façade which faced Victoria Station Drive. Because it was too small for his theatrical requirements, Youdan enlarged the building and stage by removing the old arena. He renamed it *The Alexandre Theatre and Opera House*.

After alterations, the stage was 40ft by 60ft and the seating capacity was 4,000. *The Alexandre* now had the largest stage in the provinces, which was ideal for large and lavish productions. Full scale operatic performances were often staged.

The theatre opened on 12 October 1865 with a performance of *Judas*

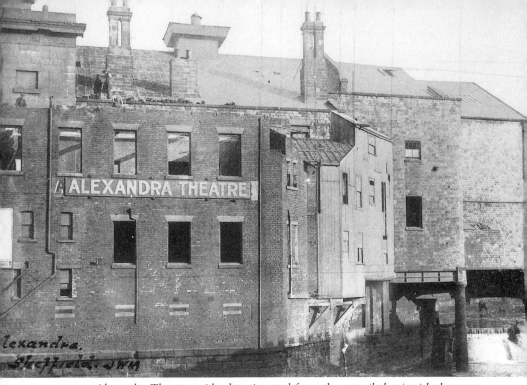

Alexandre Theatre - side elevation and from the rear, (below) with the stage backing on to the River Sheaf. Photographed in 1913.

Maccabaeus, by a flourishing Choral Union. Mr Sims, a noted singer appeared there in 1874.

The backstage area which was built on girders projected perilously out over the River Sheaf, making it a notoriously cold theatre to play during the winter. Such close proximity to the water also resulted in numerous rats entering the theatre, where they frequently pestered and terrified the chorus girls in their dressing rooms. Despite its imposing name and appearance, the theatre was known around 1870 as either *Tommy's* (after Youdan), *The Old Alex* or *The Blood Tub*! *The Alexandre* was developed to rival the *Theatre Royal* (The serious drama house).

When Youdan died in September 1883, aged 67, his House Manager, Walter Brittlebank, took control, enlarging the theatre yet again. It was now known as *The Alexandre Opera House*. (The famous Opera Company Turners appeared in 1880 and the leading lady of the company also appeared in pantomime at the theatre. Such was her popularity that patrons frequently blocked the street while waiting to enter the theatre to see her remarkable performances). Many other famous stars appeared including, J.L. Toole, Barry Sullivan, Chris Dillon, Charles Wyndham, E.S. Willard and the Misses Marie Roze and Lily Langtry, The Jersey Lily. During this period, the stage Manager was a gentleman with the notable name of Oliver Cromwell! He sported an enormous moustache and had to learn every part as principal understudy for members of the travelling companies. On one occasion, having to go on when a player failed to appear, he was very successful in the role. He was duly retained for the remainder of the season, much to the chagrin of the original actor. *The Alex* was renowned as Sheffield's Home of Pantomime, the season running from Christmas Eve to Easter. Every Shrove Tuesday, a special free matinee was staged for the elderly workhouse inmates. This was their only theatrical experience. During the intervals, gifts were handed out. Sweets and packets of tea to the ladies and tobacco to the men. In 1901, the pantomime *Robinson Crusoe* was presented starring Miss Bessie Bonehill, a leading male impersonator. In 1909, the entirely new *Dick Whittington*, the theatres forty second pantomime was staged. (In 1875 it was *Blue Beard*, again starring Mr W. and Miss Emily Randall and Tom White). During 1893, when Mr Wallace Revill took over the running of the theatre, modernisation had taken place, including electrification. The entertainments staged alternated between Grand Opera, Operettas and Plays. On the 31 January 1848, *Mr Pablo Fanque, Mazeppa and the Wild Horse*, (equestrians) and a farce *My Uncle's Card* were performed. On 3 and 4 February, the programme featured, *The Road of Life*, *The British Horseman* and *Turpin's Ride to York*. Among the memorable plays performed were *Married to the Wrong Man* and *White Slave Victim*. This bill of family entertainment rivalled *The Theatre Royal's* more serious fare, but the two theatres actually complemented each other.

The Alexandre Theatre had an elongated frontage with gabled roof sections behind. External evidence of the stage extension was the smaller gabled section to its rear. The end came for the old *Alex* in 1914 when Messrs Eadons conducted its sale. The interior appointments were sold for £300, including the pit seating which was auctioned for £19, balcony for £15 and three huge mirrors from the lounge, auctioned for £3 each. The structure was sold for £85 to Thomas Oxley of Deed Pits, for breaking up purposes on behalf of Sheffield Corporation.

The last presentation given was the play *The Bonny Pit Lad*, which was performed on 28 March 1914. By 20 May of that year, all traces of the old theatre had disappeared at the hands of the demolition workmen. Much sentimental regret attended the final demolition of the theatre, which made way for the widening of Exchange Street. However this was delayed until many years later by the intervention of the First World War. The River Sheaf which joined the River Don at this point was culverted as part of the scheme mounted in the early 1930s for the creation of Castlegate. The rebuilt *Alexandre Hotel*, (the original being opened in 1910), now stands on part of the site.

The site of the Alexandre Theatre, taken in 1999.

Act IV: A Religious Interlude

THE ALBERT HALL

Located at Barker's Pool, on the corner of Burgess Street, the former site of Quaglen's Circus. The architects were Flockton and Abbott. It had a seating capacity of 1,900 in 1912, which was decreased to 1,611 by 1935.

On 17 May 1867, a group of local Wesleyan businessmen, advised by H. Walter Ibbotson, solicitor and co-founder of the Amateur Musical Society in 1864, formed a company called, *The Sheffield Music Hall Company Limited*. This was to provide a Hall in the town centre of Sheffield for musical recitals and the presentation of various light entertainments. At a cost of £15,000, it was proposed to seat up to 3,000 people. However, it actually cost the new Music Hall Company Limited in excess of £20,000 to build this, the Wesleyan Mission Hall. The foundation stone was laid on 1 September 1870 by his Grace the Duke of Norfolk, and exactly three years later the building was complete and the official opening took place on Monday 15 December 1873. The ceremony being presided over by the Lord Mayor of Sheffield, Alderman John Hallam. The site had previously been in part, the home and shop of Ebenezer Elliott, poet and Iron and Steel merchant. He was known as the *Corn Law Rhymer*, a statue of him now stands in Weston Park. This unusual location started a trend for the migration of statues away from the city centre, to the suburbs. Externally *The Albert Hall* was an imposing edifice. In order to reduce building costs, the original plans were considerably modified resulting in a rather plain looking, sombre brick building but relieved by a series of stone arches with finial atop on the Barker's Pool elevation. The roof was flat with a looming tower with finial atop to the left, at the rear. The interior, however, was much more in keeping with the architect's original concept. The smaller hall, on the ground floor, was 48 ft long, 38 ft wide and 17 ft high. A side entrance in Burgess Street lead to the lower hall and performers accommodation.

The Great Hall was 125ft long, 60ft wide and 50ft high, with a balcony on three sides. In addition there were ten arcades together with cloakrooms, a small upper chapel and retiring rooms. The seating capacity was in fact 2,104 people, being apportioned as follows: Salon/floor; 850, orchestra; 300, upper gallery; 470, second balcony tier; 250 and balcony; 234. The stage was 37ft wide and 15ft 4″ deep, though the latter's seating capacity could be increased, by utilising the orchestra space. The company decided that, as *The Albert Hall* was to be the foremost place for entertainment in the city, an organ should be installed for concerts and musical recitals. They approached a firm in Paris owned by Monsieur Aristide Cavaille-Coll, who duly installed a magnificent and extremely large organ. It was enclosed in a beautiful oak case with front pipes of burnished tin, while it had six large bellows with unique manual blowing apparatus worked by hands and feet from below console level. The console featured Barker-lever pneumatic machines for manual and pedal action and three upper storeys of assorted components, reached by two well-finished spiral staircases concealed behind the two 16ft case towers. A *grand orgue wind ventil pedal*, admitted wind to the whole of

the great organ's 4,082 *tuyaux de L'orgue* (pipes). The whole of the workmanship, interior and exterior was of the very highest order and cost approximately £5,500. But reputedly, Cavaille-Coll still lost money on the contract. With its 76 stops, this organ was considered to be one of the finest in England (it was once played by Alexander Guilmani). The principal entrance was from Barker's Pool with a stairway on each side of the spacious entrance hall, one leading to the great hall corridors; the other, the balcony and galleries. The interior design was very opulent, walls and ceiling being adorned with fine panels and rich tracery carving with famous composers names engraved above and intricate designs of cornucopia and Doric columns. Flanking the organ were two curved boxes, arched and suitably draped. Two beautiful and ornate chandeliers hung above. The 'orchestra' in

The Albert Hall seating plan.

The Albert Hall, Barkers Pool.

front of the organ was for occupation of concert musicians, providing additional seating for the audience on other occasions. The term 'Music Hall', implied that the Hall was for concert use and it was not licensed as a variety theatre. The secretary of *The Albert Hall* was Mr J.W. Peace and if you wanted information about the forthcoming presentations then you telephoned 563!

The first performance at *The Albert Hall* was Handel's *Messiah* conducted by Mr R.S. Burton of Leeds. From that day forward the Hall was Sheffield's principal concert centre. An *Albert Choral Society* of 100 voices was formed in 1877 under Mr T. Tallis Trimnell, with the support of the gentlemen's committee who felt that a choral society had long been needed in the town. Apart from promenade concerts, brass band competitions and Operas, the Hall was also used for political and general public meetings. The fine Cavaille-Coll organ, was not originally tuned to standard concert pitch (C440). It was re-tuned bringing it into line with English orchestras. This operation required substancial expenditure. Mr E Willoughby-Firth paid for this work and in return the directors offered the festival association free use of the hall on three ocasions. The first music festival in 1896 included eight local choral societies consisting of 300 voices. They combined to perform *Elijah*, and *The Damnation of Faust*. Due to its success on Friday 13 October 1899, the second of the triennial music festivals was held.

Artistes appearing included: Miss Clara Butt. Composers, Edward Elgar and Sir C Hubert H Parry, conducted their own works, respectively King Olaf and King Saul. Mr August Manns conducted the augmented Crystal Palace Orchestra, as he did in 1896. As a result of the excellent quality of performance and the fine acoustics, these festivals played to packed houses and had a devoted following.

Over the years, the entertainments were varied and many. Lord Randloph Churchill and Lord Baden-Powell, founder of the Scout Movement, both visited here. There were a series of concerts linked with William Brown, e.g. *The Black Face and Midget Minstrels*, some of which were augmented with magic lantern shows. Remarkable effects were achieved and 'living pictures' were only a step away from being launched at such a concert on 5 September, 1896. Advertised as 'demonstrating' Mr Bert Acres 'kineoptican' new wonder of the world, film selections included *The Derby*, *Feeding a Tiger* and *Finsbury Park Railway Station*. This presentation was supported by variety artistes, and popular music was a regular feature of the Hall's programme. Occasionally, the programmes were of a religious nature or concerned some current topic. For example depicting a Royal Occasion or the Boer War! From 17 to 22 October 1921, The Grand Opera Society of

The Albert Hall interior showing the Cavaille-Coll Organ.

Sheffield and District presented Verdi's operas *Aida* and *Faust*. Albert Parker appeared playing the chimes, wine glasses and bottles!, while Loie Freeman of 'The Midgets' also played here. This was before he became a big musical comedy star. At the turn of the century, a primitive form of moving pictures was touring the country's Halls, known as Charles W. Poole's Myriorama. A typical 'Eventographe' programme from circa 1899, included *Cairo to Fashoda, America and Spain, Lovely Venice* and *Spectacular Volcanic Eruption*, all colourful depictions of the world. Live support acts included *Boswells Drawing Room Circus* with educated ponies and equestrian dogs, *Tissot's Marionettes* and *Mandolin and Orchestral and Military Band*. The Myriorama consisted of transformation scenes and moving tableaux with sound effects traditionally playing The *Albert Hall* in 1910. Similarly, *Hamiltons Panorama* was also presented. This circus styled presentation featured overhead trapeze artistes crossing the hall to accompanying music performed by a big band, while spectacular effects took place on stage. Many accidents occurred between the audience and hurtling artistes, due to the inadequacy of the safety precautions at the time. *Dysons Diorama*, was a combination of Swiss choir and films.

Some of the world's most famous singers and instrumentalists appeared, including Madame Adelina Patti, who said it was the easiest Hall she ever sang in, among others, Madame Tetrazzini and Charles Halle also appeared. *Dyson's Gypsy Choir* sang here too. At Christmas time, children were enchanted with seasonal shows featuring circus acts. In addition, there were famous organists and resident first rate orchestras. In 1878, a great meeting of working men was addressed in the Hall by the Archbishop of York. There was even a flying visit from 'The Spelling Bees' at weekends, held by the headmaster of Brunswick School, Mr Greenup. On Saturday 24 April 1915, the Musicians Union held a concert in aid of the Wounded War Soldiers Fund. Father Ignatius, a Welsh monk, drew in the crowds to evangelistic meetings. Similarly, the American evangelists Moody and Sankey of Chicago, also used the hall.

The hall was an ideal venue for the early pioneers to exhibit the new wondrous animated pictures. When King Edward VII visited the city on 12 July 1905, to open the University, Frank Mottershaw's Sheffield Photo Company showed a film of the event the same evening. Films with crude sound were exhibited by Sydney Carter's *Gaumont Chronophone* for a month in 1906, with weekly programme changes. The main hall was leased to *North British Animated Pictures* and the opening programme was *Babes in the Wood* (in colour), *Billy's Christmas Turkey* and *Her Darkest Hour*, on 19 December. An orchestra played during the 3.00pm and 8.00pm performances. Admission was 6d, 9d and 1/-. A publicised film *The Queen of Sheba,* played on 25 January 1913. However, film presentations were sporadic because of Sunday closing enabling the Hall to be used for religious services. An agreement between company and owners permitted daily film performances except when the Hall was booked for the established programme of concerts, meetings and conferences. This stop-go arrangement militated against the establishment of regular patronage and was compounded by a hall closure for six weeks in June, ostensibly for cleaning!

The last presentation was *Tess of the Durbevilles,* which closed on 24 January 1914. Minor structural alteration had been required to facilitate the provision of a projection box and rewind room. The mind boggles at the inadequate facilities countenanced for the presentation of films during the last sixteen years that the Hall was open! A number of external alterations had been made to the building since it opened. In 1896, a canopy was erected on cantilevers above the Burgess Street entrance. In 1905, all the sanitary amenities were improved. Seating capacity was much reduced after 1893, with the large hall seating 1900. However this was greatly reduced when an orchestra played and pictures were projected on the screen. Mid-way through the First World War, *The Albert Hall* must have been a very large white elephant to its owners. Wartime difficulties caused concert cancellations and for much of 1914-1918, the film showings were severely restricted. Poole's *Myriorama* returned in November 1914, showing pictures of the war *From The Front.* 1915-1916 saw only four films available for showing over the Christmas and New Year period.

D.W. Griffith's *Intolerance* had its Sheffield premiere on 3 December 1917. The situation improved and films played more regularly during 1918. On Monday 17 June 1918 the propaganda film, *The Kaiser, Beast of Berlin* was shown. Afterwards the Hall operated almost continuously as a cinema, greatly alleviating war-weariness for the patrons and operators of the Hall. Even though there was a renewed interest in choralism, proposals were put forward for permanent cinema conversion. By 1915, the owners had declared a deficit and on 7 February 1916, it was decided to sell *The Albert Hall* due to inadequate support by the public of musical entertainments. This outraged music lovers, as T. Walter Hall pointed out, the Hall was not perfect, but it was the only suitable venue for festivals, choral and orchestral concerts. In April 1918, the city council declined to purchase *The Albert Hall* on the grounds of its seating limitations. The Council had on hand a proposal to erect a new hall seating 4,000 on an alternative site!

In 1918 the owners decided to lease the property to a Leeds based company, *New Century Pictures,* who had exhibited at the Hall back in

1906. In 1919, *The Albert Hall* was sold to *New Century Pictures*, who ran it with enthusiasm. With regard to admission prices; in 1918, they were structured to establish *The Albert Hall* as a cinema with a regular audience. At the time the comparatively expensive seat costs of, 1/- Saloon, 2/4 Front Balcony, 1/6 Balcony tier, 1/3 Side Balcony, reflected the novelty of the cinema at that time. Use as a permanent cinema with regular audiences gave *The Albert Hall* a new lease of life and a series of improvements were undertaken. commencing in May 1919. For the next sixteen months, extensive alteration work was undertaken. A proscenium was erected and new curtains were added to reduce the stage width. A new projection box was built and the projectors replaced with modern equipment. The Hall was redecorated and the seating capacity increased and ventilation was improved with the installation of a large fan. An original proposal to construct a dress circle, was however abandoned. Following these improvements, a silent movie starring, Anna Pavlova, celebrated ballet dancer, was presented as *The Worlds Greatest Picture*, and was promoted by the use of billboard, notice boards, sandwich boards and even posters mounted upon a horse drawn cart!

In 1921, more practical sanitary facilities were constructed, making them more accessible to those in the gallery. In 1924, an adaptation with the use of mirrors made it possible for the organist to see both the screen and musical director. This overcame a problem created by the recent stage alterations. Also in that year, rocket lights, coloured to catch the eye, were erected on top of the building. The basement was also altered, to provide covered waiting accommodation for patrons in an undercover area equipped with good lighting and ventilation. The Hall was closed on 13 June 1927 for a major renovation including extensive internal and external alterations. The architects in charge of these alterations were Chadwick and Weston, of Leeds.

A new canopy was erected along the entire front and side of the building providing shelter for 1,500 people. The foyers was remodelled in Grecian style with extensive use of marble and a three way mahogany pay box in the centre. Another new proscenium arch increased the stage depth by ten feet, previously it was very shallow. The interior of the Hall was refurbished in shades of blue, gold and cream. A Holophic, lighting system was also installed. This created multi-coloured effects, including a prismatic colouring of the screen curtains. An improved ventilation system was also installed with new ladies sanitary facilities at circle level. It was not planned to increase the seating capacity, which remained at 1,611. The organ was modernised, since it was not of course a cinema organ. (Early in 1920, the pitch had been lowered to blend better with the orchestra). It was in regular use during the silent film era and for organ recitals during the interludes, following the introduction of talking pictures. Organists included, Sydney Lamb, J.W. Stricklan, George Vergil Dawson and Harold Dring. During the modernisation, the combination pedals were removed plus the addition of sixteen thumb pistons and nine pistons. Performances were matinee and evening weekday but from 1920, the programme was continuous from 2.00pm.

A fourteen piece orchestra accompanied the film presentations. In 1924, Mr Cherry Kearton appeared for one week to discuss his animal films, which were being presented at the time.

Re-opening on 25 February 1927, *The Albert Hall* now became the self styled 'Temple of the Motion Picture', showing more films than the majority of its Sheffield competitors. The programmes were both varied and exciting! *The Ten Commandments*, *The Merry Widow* (1925), *Ben Hur* (It's Sheffield premier being in 1928). *Mamba* (1930), *Becky Sharp*, the first feature film made entirely in the then new, three colour 'Technicolor', process was shown in November 1935. By 1928, New Century Pictures was controlled by the *Gaumont British Picture Corporation*, who took over the Hall in March of that year. They installed as manager, Mr R Rea.

As late as 1929, vocalists and occasional variety acts accompanied the feature films. there were also personal appearances by various celebrities of the day. Ivor Novello, of *The Dancing Years*, *Perchance to Dream* and *King's Rhapsody* fame, appeared to promote his film, *Man Without Desire*. A naval commander introduced from the stage the feature film, *Q Ships*. However, programmes lost most of the trimmings, with the advent of talking pictures.

In March 1929, the Wesleyan Mission, who had always held religious services on Sundays at *The Albert Hall*, were finally asked to find another venue. Even as a cinema, the balmy days of the Hall were over and it was playing second fiddle to the adjacent *Regent Cinema*.

The first 'Talkie', entitled *Weary River*, starring Richard Barthelmess, played the week of 9 September 1929 and was programmed with a silent film, *Detectives*.

The sound system installed at *The Albert Hall* was the Western Electric system, *The Albert Hall* being the third Sheffield cinema to convert to sound after the *Regent* and the *Picture House*.

She Wanted a Millionaire, starring Joan Bennet, played during 1932, but times were changing and *The Albert Hall* was not keeping pace. On the 14 July 1937, what was to be *The Albert Hall's* last ever film was shown. Starring Humphrey Bogart and Dick Foran and ironically entitled *Black Legion*. A premonition of things to come.

A serious fire broke out on the night of 14 July, probably starting about ten minutes after the end of the evening performance. The attendants were still locking up and the manager Reg Rea was still in his office when the alarm was raised. The fire brigade was called immediately and fought hard to save the building, especially at the point where the forty foot high rear stage tower which opened onto the roof, threatened to collapse. It was feared that this might set fire to the nearby *Regent Cinema* and other adjoining properties.

Soon after the fire started, its red glow could be seen as far away as Millhouses. The firemen had even doused the interior with water jets from hoses mounted atop a ninety foot escape ladder, but all their efforts were of no avail. The flames totally gutted the Hall and also destroyed the great Cavaille-Coll organ, which had only recently been sealed up behind the cinema screen. By the morning of 15 July the fire had been extinguished and the façade appeared little affected. Large crowds gathered in the area of Barker's Pool to witness the end of this grand old lady of Sheffield's stage and screen, *The Albert Hall*. At one point the crowd was estimated to be some 10,000 people.

The blackened shell of the building remained standing for some years, after being made safe before eventual demolition. The site was cleared amidst proposals to erect a new cinema on the site. Designs were presented by architect Mr W. E. Trent, but they were not pursued and the new cinema never materialised. The site was eventually purchased by the

Photographed in 1999, The Cole Brothers Department Store now stands where The Albert Hall once stood.

Corporation after the Second World War, as the intended site for the new Law Courts. These plans also came to nothing and in 1963, Cole Brothers built a store on the site.

Footnotes:

From 1350 onwards, all the Sheffield town buildings were constructed of timber framed walls with thatched roofs. Clearly, this was a dangerous and potentially fatal fire hazard.

Barker's Pool was so named when in 1434, a Mr Barker, of Balm Green, created the first artificial water storage reservoir for the benefit of the citizens of the town. The town depended upon the reservoir for firefighting purposes, and as a constant supply of pure drinking water. The source of supply was springs in the West Bar hills. The reservoir was an oblong walled space 36 yards long and 20 yards wide. It was re-constructed in 1631 by Robert Rollynson and further enlarged during 1672-74. On one occasion in 1654, it was used in conjunction with the cucking stool for the ducking of termagents.

This was the town's highest point and reputedly, damage to the reservoir caused severe flooding in the town. The reservoir, by then regarded as a nuisance, was filled in during 1773.

In 1940, during the Blitz, A bomb exploded and severely damaged the roadway in Barker's Pool. Chuncks of flying shrapnel scarred the Regent Cinema and City Hall stonework. Evidence of this event can still be seen on the City Hall frontage pillars.

During the 1930's, there had been discussions about the possibility of removing the organ, complete with it's new screen console, from The Albert Hall and installing it in the new City Hall which was then under construction. However, nothing came of the proposal and The Albert Hall fire sealed it's fate.

At one time, The Albert Hall basement contained the Sheffield branch of N.A.L.G.O. indoor games centre.

In February 1978, three tickets dated 1895, for The Albert Hall, were discovered behind a skirting board at the home of a Mr H. Stainland, in Nether Edge, Sheffield.

Curiously, there is a photograph of The Albert Hall in the magazine Kinematograph Weekly, publicising the film Fire. This was however, in 1928, some nine years prior to the event.

Act V: The Dream Palaces

THE EMPIRE PALACE OF VARIETIES

L ocated on Union Street, with a frontage in Charles Street, at the corner with Union Street. The proprietors were The Sheffield Empire Palace Limited, part of the Moss and Thornton Syndicate Empire chain of theatres. It consisted of:

Managing Directors: Messrs H.E. Moss and (Sir) Oswald Stoll. (1886-1942)
President Director: Mr R Thornton.
General Manager: Mr Frank Allen.
Acting Manager: Mr J. Pelloe.
Treasurer: Mr J. Whittle
Architect: Mr Frank Matcham.

It first opened in 1895, on the site previously occupied by the Alhambra Theatre at a cost of £65,000, boasting a seating capacity of 3,000, with standing room for another 1,000.

The extremely tasteful and effective frontage was of brick and stone decorated with handsome mouldings. The words 'Empire Palace', adorned the top pediment which capped the centre being heavily carved and surmounted by the figure of a boy, carrying a flambeau with other figures at his feet representing music, with a flagpole atop. Two arched alcoves with bottom stone 'Jacobean', spindles and with inset windows flanked a central opening with smaller pediment and finial above, also with an inset window and circular stone lattice above. Two arched stone structures with finials and stone 'Jacobean', spindles

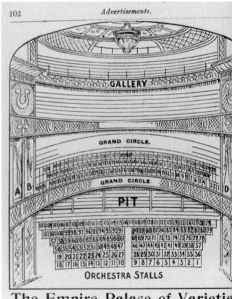

The Empire Palace of Varietie

TWO PERFORMANCES NIGHTLY at 7 and 9.   Doors open 6-15 and 8
PRICES:—Private Boxes, to hold four, 7/6; extra seats, 2/- each. Orchestra b
reserved, 1/6.   Grand Circle, reserved, 1/3, unreserved, 1/-.   Pit (tip-up chairs
Gallery (upholstered, 3d.
THE EMPIRE PALACE OF VARIETIES, in PINSTONE-STREET, is a hand
structure to accommodate 3,500 people, erected at a cost of £65,000, with a
latest improvements, sliding roof, electric light; fire proof curtain, &c., &c. T
is a circle and gallery, with stalls and pit, all handsomely furnished. Proprie
Moss's Empires Limited.   Chairman, Mr. H. E. Moss ; managing director
Oswald Stoll; assistant director and chief of staff, Mr. Frank Allen ; res
manager, Mr. Alan D. Dunbar.

A seating plan of The Empire Palace.

The Empire Theatre, Charles Street, before façade alteration.

Two views of the auditorium taken from the stage of The Empire Theatre in 1950s.

adjoining the centre pediment were topped with copper domes and finials. The Mensard roof of the entrance vestibules was seen above this pediment and crowned with prettily decorated iron work. The carving on the façade, included numerous subjects in harmony with the purposes to which the building was devoted. The shelter at the entrance, was closed at night by ornamental iron gates, situated above two small steps. A magnificent theatre, indeed of an opulence not previously seen in Sheffield. In later years the extensive frontage was further altered with the erection of a long glass canopy over the entrance doors with 'Empire Palace', on a curved central panel with 'Empire', in bolder lettering at an angle to either side. Imposing street lamps stood at each end of the new canopy. By 1941, this had been replaced by a straight ended, flat fronted canopy which also housed the presentation display. 'Empire' illuminated letter signs were placed in the two arches and the street furniture had gone. In later years, the central opening had either a display board for the presentations or a small 'V' shaped, double sided 'Empire' sign projecting from the façade halfway between the canopy and finialed pediment. The Union Street elevation consisted of a long ornamental façade with exit doors beneath windows crowned with pediments. Beyond these were three arches with pedimented windows having an imposing larger pediment in the centre on the roof line. There were further windows beyond with the stage door beneath. Beyond the mensard roof was an elongated roof with ceiling opening framework and behind this a sloping roof with ventilation dome atop. In addition there were four tall chimneys.

The Box Office ran alongside the theatre entrance with a large display window for playbills. Inside, at one end, was a full-length counter with three grilled pay windows, like a bank. Current, next and forthcoming attractions occupied one window each. Inside the auditorium was truly a 'Palace of Delight'. Looking from the stage, the roof rose 68 feet from the orchestra pit to the ceiling. The hexagonal ceiling was in fibrous plaster decorated with subjects and figures representing Music and Art, relieved with short pillars and arches. In the centre of this elaborate and effective ceiling, was an octagon lantern roof upon latticed girders, which provided admirable ventilation by sliding open in hot weather to cool the theatre and in addition efficiently removed tobacco fumes and bad air. This opening roof was a feature of the building. The circle was horse-shoe shaped and decorated in fibrous plaster embossed with 'egg-shaped', raised relief panels spaced regularly along its frontage, each being adorned with 'shell-like', flanks and a crowned female figure above. Directly between each one were triple drop-lamps of fluted shape, between ornamentation of swirls and swags.

The gallery was similarly executed but with rectangular panels with

View of the stage and auditorium in the 1950s.

swags between Tudor rose decorations flanking the lamps. The circle and gallery were supported by eight pillars, the two nearest the stage being decorated in the Corinthian style with ornamental capitals. Four small vauted arches at circle level flanked a larger central one with 'Jacobean' spindles above, divided by ornamental pairs of cherubs bearing laurels and sceptres. Stalls, circle and gallery all had exit doors at the rear sides. On either side of the auditorium at circle level were two adjacent boxes, each with bulbous fronts decorated with swirls and a large tudor rose. The rose also being the central feature of a heavily ornamented circular panel. They were arched at gallery level being divided by decorated pillars with pear drop panels and ornamentation above. The arches were decorated with six dividing wedges with a heavily ornamented balustrade above swirling pediments supporting a lyre with laurel swags which made an attractive top feature. The ceiling had an elaborate fitting with drop shades surrounding the octagon.

The proscenium arch was square, the sides having flat fronted panels with an inner angled edge and ornamental relief. The outer edge was right angled with a heavily decorated moulded border of rope-like effect. The centre was adorned with a large 'egg-shaped', relief panel executed with frolicking cherubs holding musical instruments. It was edged with a heavy ornamental pattern of swirls with a pair of cherubs bearing laurels and sceptres, which matched those at ceiling level. At either side was a female statue sitting on a swirl edged seat, reading a book. Below the central panel was a balustrade topped with a large ornamental swag of laurel with 'Music' engraved on a rectangular panel. At circle level, on either side, adjoining the boxes was another elaborate exit with relief panel and portico above a panelled door. Decorative mirrors hung at either side. The ground floor was reached from either the main entrance in Charles Street or from Union Street.

There were six rows of orchestral stalls with luxuriously upholstered tip-up seats. These were divided from the seven rows of pit stalls with the ordinary pit seats behind. At either side were promenades leading to a smoking room and lounge behind the seats. Staircases on either side, near the proscenium, lead to the next tier forming the dress and upper circle and the two boxes at either side. Covered corridors ran round, opening into the crush bar and lavatories and the inner vestibule of the main entrance. These apartments were under the upper part of the dress circle, which also had the luxuriously upholstered tip-up seats. At the back of the latter was a spacious open promenade and 'slips', or walks at the sides from which the entertainment could be seen. Behind the promenade was a very handsome smoking room and lounge. The next tier consisted of the galleries, which were divided into upper and lower. The same staircase from the vestibule lead to both. There were open 'slips' at the sides reaching nearly to the proscenium. The galleries also had entrances from Union Street and was fitted with wooden bench seats. The boxes and arches above were adorned with luxurious drapes which were fastened back for dramatic effect, with ornate trimmed pelmets above. The proscenium curtains were of similar design, also being drawn back and had top swags with a central inverted 'fan-shaped', drop. The plasterwork throughout the auditorium was finished in steel and burnished gold with a touch of other harmonising colours for the relief of eye fatigue! When the electric light glared out fully, it gave this blaze of gold an entrancing palace appearance. During renovation in later years, for increased comfort in keeping with changing social values, many features of the auditorium were altered. The box arches were filled in, with panels of an intertwined thistle and leaves design and the lyres atop removed. The proscenium 'shells', vanished as did the circle exit mirrors. The box drapes were replaced with very plain ones, with flat pelmets as were the proscenium curtains, having a lowered panel with scalloped fringing and rectangular trims with tassels. All the stalls promenades were removed and the entire seating was converted to upholstered, tip-up seating. The original handsome lighting was replaced. The circle and gallery façades had new single drop lamps of hexagonal design and the ceiling supported six larger hexagonal lamps with two tier shades and scalloped 'bowls' above.

The new theatre was, without doubt magnificent, being equipped with the very latest gadgets and electric light and the 'Gods' smiled down from the heavens. Shortly after the theatre was completed, the 'Empire' buildings were erected to the left on the corner of Union Street and on the right on Charles Street and facing Pinstone Street. An imposing edifice, it had a row of shops on the ground floor (notably 'Richards and Company', milliners and drapers), with three storeys above. Impressive roof windows with pediments and finials flanked a smaller structure also with finialed pediment. At the corner was a similar one engraved '1895'. The development of Pinstone Street was soon completed, with the erection of a further seven shops and a restaurant in Charles Street opposite the theatre. Grand Opening Night was on Monday 4 November 1895, and the opening Variety Bill included Miss Cora Stuart and Company in *The Fair Equestrienne*. This celebrated sketch was presented with a supporting company including: Oakland and Thompson (the accomplished operatic duettists), Spry and Austin (in their amusing comedy act), Lottie Lynne (serio comedienne), Bernard Armstrong (eccentric comedian and dancer), F. W. Mills (the great Australian ventriloquist) and Nellie Christie (the original 'female' Dandy coloured coon). The Frantz Family Acrobats performed their stunning display in full evening dress! *The Empire* Orchestra of twenty instrumentalists was under the leadership of Mr Ralph Booth.

Admission prices were as follows: Private boxes £1 11s 6d, Fauteuils 2/-, Grand Circle 1/6d, Upper Circle and Promenade 1/-, Pit Stalls 9d, Pit and Amphitheatre 6d and Gallery 4d. The performance commenced at 7.30pm.

Long before this time, shouts of *'standing room only'*, warned latecomers of the perils of delay. After the show, the Manager spoke from the stage with regard to the standard of continued excellence the patrons could expect from future presentations, and the architect, Mr Matcham wished the new *Empire Theatre* every success. Which it was, a huge success with many famous names appearing over the years that followed and the presentation of chiefly first rate variety with the occasional play or musical interlude.

In 1896, the manager was Arthur Holmes who began his career as 'Professor Holmes' the conjuror, then 'Olmas' the trapeze artist and champion plate spinner. (He was in the first circus act to visit South Africa, in 1877).

On 6 April 1896, Miss Vesta Tilley came to the *Empire Theatre*. She was known as 'The London Idol' and specialised in male impersonation. Her act was fantastically popular, making her 'a setter of male fashion and improver of the Hall's morality'. She later married Sir Walter de Frece. Little Tich appeared on 15 June. His real name was Harry Relph. He was a 'big boot dancer', wearing long wooden soled boots with which he would leap in the air and land on the tips. (Sir) George Robey, also appeared on 21 September, that year. He also played the *Empire Theatre* on 4 February 1929. Miss Florrie Forde appeared on 16 May 1898, and much later on Monday 19 September 1938. The 'Famous Principal Boy' she immortalised the song *'Down at the Old Bull and Bush'*.

Mr Fred Karno's Company appeared on 24 July 1899, (note; including Earnest Parsons, tumbler and juggler, great uncle of the publisher). The company included Charles Chaplin and Stan Jefferson (later Laurel) in 'Mumming Birds'. Then aged nineteen, Chaplin played a red nosed drunk in white tie and tails! 25 September 1899, saw the presentation of *'The American Biograph'*, showing the court martial of Captain Dreyfuss at Rennfy. Around this period, Talbot O' Farrell appeared at the *Empire Theatre*. A Scottish comedian and singer, he became a stage Irishman and his signature tune was *'That Old Fashioned Mother of Mine'*. When Miss Marie Lloyd played the *Empire* on 13 August 1900 she had the rare experience of being booed by the audience, 'Our Marie, Queen of the Halls', promptly told the audience where they could stick their knives, scissors and circular saws! Undeterred, she continued to sing '*Oh, Mr Porter*', with her usual risque style and suggestive winks! She first appeared on stage as Bella Delamore at the *Eagle Music Hall*, London in 1855. The famous illusionist 'Chung Ling Soo', real name William Ellsworth Robinson!, (1861-1918) played the *Empire* on 24 March 1902. Billed as the 'Chinese Magician Extraordinary', he used to 'fish', over the audience and 'catch' live goldfish. (He was killed in 1918, under strange circumstances when his 'catching bullets on a plate', trick went drastically wrong. He was mortally wounded as a result). Harry Houdini, real name Ehrich Weiss, (1874 - 1926), appeared on 25 April 1904. An amazing escapologist, he would escape from handcuffs and steel bound boxes.

Chung Ling Soo, Chinese magician extraordinary.

The first documented presentation of 'animated pictures', was on 22 June 1896. This was using the 'Variety Lumiere Cinematographe', the programme included variety artiste J.E. Camp, comedian and the then famous, 'Lavater's Dog Orchestra'. When King Edward VII came to visit Sheffield on 12 July 1905, as previously mentioned, the event was filmed.

The *Empire Theatre* competed with the *Albert Hall*, in showing this royal visit on a variety bill which stated '*H.R.H. The King's visit to Sheffield, will be photographed and reproduced the same evening on the American Bioscope*'. The entertainment offered by the *Empire*, included 'The Four Jumels', 'May Milburn' and 'Mills and Rawlins', two Sheffield favourites in a comedy oddity.

The Box Office opened daily from 10.00am to 4.00pm. Telephone bookings could be made by dialling 603!

On 4 December 1905, Miss Nellie Wallace (1870-1948) came to the theatre. A serio-comedienne, with her feather boa, sniffle and suggestive wink, she topped Music Hall Bills for many years. She returned to the *Empire* on 4 February 1935, in '*Laughter Zone*', which also featured a galaxy of beautiful girls. Nellie presented an entirely new collection of comedy characters, in addition to her 'character', songs. In 1948, she appeared with five other Music Hall greats in '*Thanks for the Memory*'.

Miss Hettie King was reputed to be the world's greatest, immaculate, male impersonator, particularly in nautical disguise. She played the *Empire* on 8 April 1907, Monday 25 July 1932 and Monday 14 August 1939.

Sir Harry Lauder, the famous Scottish singing comedian. (1870-1950)

On the 16 September 1907, Sir Harry Lauder, (1870 - 1950), the famous Scottish singing comedian who was billed as 'The Laird of the Halls', played at the theatre and again on Monday 2 October 1931. On each occasion he was supported by a star variety company.

'La Milo', real name Pansy Montage, who was originally from Australia, toured the Halls giving 'exhibitions of statuary', Andromeda, Lady Godiva, the Velasquez Venus, Bacchante etc, and she was sometimes accused of indecency. However, nobody complained when members of Sheffield Watch Committee saw her act at the *Empire* in 1907 and 1908!

Mr Seymour Hicks and Miss Zena Dare played the theatre on 21 June 1909. Miss Ada Reeve, real name Adelaide Mary Isaacs, (1874 - 1966), appeared on 13 June 1910 and later on Monday 14 August 1939. She was a celebrated comedy actress of great talent and beauty.

George Formby, played the *Empire* on 22 August 1910. He used to sing '*I Was Standing at the Corner of the Street*'. This was the father of the famous ukulele playing George Formby Junior.

From 24 December 1910, Mr Fred Kitchen, a favourite Sheffield comedian presented, for the second time at the *Empire* that year, his big success 'Private Potts' a military comedy. On 24 April 1911, the legendary Mr W.C. Fields appeared at the theatre. Mr G.H. Elliott (George Henry 1884-1962), came to the *Empire* on 18 September 1911 and much later in his career on Monday 19 August 1946. Billed as 'The Chocolate Coloured Coon' he carried a Gladstone bag with 'Frys Chocolate' emblazoned on it. A magical black-face artiste, his famous song was '*I used to sigh for the Silvery Moon*', half sung, half yodelled with soft shoe dancing.

Mr Fred Emney (1865 - 1917), played the theatre on 26 August 1912. His act included his famous 'Dame', sketch '*A Sister to Assist Her!*'.

The thought of 'The Divine Sarah', working the Halls is mind boggling, but the drama came to Sheffield with the appearance of Madame Sarah Bernhardt who played a single matinee on Tuesday 5

(Above) Miss Ellaline Terriss and Mr Seymour Hicks.

(Right) Mrs Ada Reeve, a comedy actress. (1874-1966).

November 1912. By then, in her late 60s she was still able to portray every mood in a thirty minute scene. The theatre was packed from floor to ceiling, such was the popularity of this celebrated actress. She was paid £1,000 per week in gold. After each performance she would receive a proportionate sum. For the duration of her appearance, her dressing suite was redecorated and a rich red carpet laid to her place of performance on the stage. This was a peculiarity of hers, to avoid walking where any performing animals might have trod, since she despised the then frequent cruelty employed in their training. This celebrated actress was famous for 'The Lady of the Camelias'. In later life, despite the amputation of one leg, she still played the theatres. Unable to wear an artificial limb, she remained seated throughout her entire performance. Despite this handicap she still achieved great, dramatic effect with her hand gestures and marvellous voice in suitable playlets, a remarkable Tour De Force. She passed away in 1923.

For one week only, from Monday 30 December 1912, Mr John Tiller's famous pantomime 'Cinderella', was presented starring Mary Brougham in the title role and Ethel Negretti as 'Prince Charming'. During its history, the Empire staged no less than nine productions of this, the most popular pantomime of its day. At this time the Empire Theatre was billed as 'the most comfortable in Sheffield', and on Monday 27 January 1913, there was an appearance of 'The Elliott Savonas', England's Musical Marvels. This family of eight instrumentalists performed 'The Palace of Orpheus', on a variety bill which also included Will Hay 'The Original Schoolmaster Comedian'. Admission prices were around 2d to 1/6d.

Dr Walford (Sam) Bodie MD came to the Empire on 4 August 1913. He was an electrical illusionist who claimed that the self styled 'MD', stood for Merry Devil! As promised by the management, the standard of presentations was replete with all that was excellent, refined and entertaining! The Empire Theatre prospered and as soon as patrons entered its magic portals, they were hooked. They came, they saw and they were conquered. This was truly a Palace of Varieties with its red plush, sparkling brass and pink cherubs gazing down onto the stage below. The Empire stage measured 66ft wide by 30ft deep and was fitted so that it was quickly alterable to suit the needs of play or pantomime, at short notice. Backstage there were dressing rooms on several floors, paint rooms, prop rooms, lavatories and a Manager's room. The stage itself had bridges, traps, slides and good sized wings. Additional exits were provided for emergency use in case of fire and there was an easily accessible escape ladder from the flies in the stage tower above. A large engine house and emergency dynamo were also installed, when the agreement to provide electricity for the theatre was accepted by the Electric Light and Power Company. Heating of the theatre was done by a hot water system. For the total safety of the patrons, exits were placed all over the building for efficient evacuation, if required. The crush rooms and other busy parts of the theatre, were constructed from iron and cement to make them fireproof. Every possible means were taken to prevent the outbreak of fire and to avoid loss of life if such an unfortunate event should occur, which considering the events of the next four years, was quite a possibility. During the First World War the Empire continued to flourish with its twice nightly variety shows. The competition it created initially, on its opening and ever since, resulted in decline and fall for the West Bar theatreland. Catering for the masses at popular prices, the Empire had naturally taken much of their custom. The Grand, West Bar, promptly introduced the two performances a night policy, to compete and had forced the *Empire* to follows suit. Unintentionally, they had created a new style of presentation!

The variety shows comprised of an opening line of chorus girls, speciality acts and a finale being either singer or comedian but usually a top of the bill Music Hall star.

On Monday 7 June 1915, the presentation was '*Here We Are Again*', in three scenes, starring John Humphries, the famous comedian with Mona Magnet and George Law. This musical burlesque bill also included the latest news and war newsreels, along with 'Vernon Watson', the popular London mimic. Telephone bookings could be made by dialling 682!

On the bright moonlit night of 26 September 1915, there was an enemy air attack. Just before 10.00pm, citizens living beyond the city's southern boundaries heard a loud, droning sound approaching, coming from an enormous cigar shaped German Zeppelin as it cruised majestically towards Sheffield, following the railway lines from the south

George Robey and family (1869-1954).

which were shining brightly. It moved steadily northwards and soon
bombs were dropped on Sheffield, in Stanley Street, Pitsmoor, near The
Wicker. This was followed by the glare of fires from the destroyed houses
in which twenty eight people were killed. At the *Empire Theatre* which
as usual had a capacity crowd, the audience were enjoying George
Robey. His trade mark was huge eyebrows and a clergyman's coat.
Shortly before the end of his song, which had the verses ending in '*Aw
shurrup!*', the drone of the engines of the approaching Zeppelin was
heard and it seemed likely that it would pass over or very near the packed
theatre. There was a gasp of fear throughout the audience, which quickly
edged towards panic. George Robey stopped singing, listened quizzically
to the rapidly increasing overhead noise and then waived a derisive arm
towards the roof, shouting in a tone of disgust '*Aw Shurrup!*' The whole
audience shared a burst of laughter which dispelled any feelings of panic
and the still giggling crowd made a leisurely, unperturbed exit. He
appeared at the *Empire* again from Monday 4 February 1929, with an
entirely new production '*In Other Words*', with Marie Blanche, 'The
Hippodrome Eight', 'The Five Jewels' and 'The Gypsy Quintett'.
Performances were unusually once nightly with Thursday matinee and
Friday at 8.00pm. Manager of the theatre at this time was Mr A.H. Williams.
    Mr Shaun Glenville (1884 - 1968), and his wife, Dorothy Ward,
appeared at the theatre on 17 May 1915 and on Monday 15 October
1923. The two Sheffield favourites appeared in a variety bill with Tom
D. Newell, 'The Two Fishers' and Lawrence Tiller's 'Dorothy Dots'. Mr
Glenville's character portrayal was of a fellow of infinite jocularity, while
Miss Ward wore a marvellous array of gorgeous dresses. In 1944, they
starred in the pantomime '*Jack and the Beanstalk*', Mr Bertram
Montague's second Christmas presentation. On this occasion they played
mother and son, Dame and Jack Durden, with Gay and Gay as 'Donald
and Pluto'. Specialities were presented by 'The Six Mighty Atoms' and
Ronnie Dukes, (aged 15), with the juvenile dancing girls. Ronnie found
fame much later, with Miss Ricki Lee as the duo 'Dukes and Lee'.
Costumes for this production were by L and H Nathan Limited. This was
Miss Ward's favourite pantomime with varying line deliveries from her
husband at each performance, as a result of his reputed partaking of a
drop or two of the sherbet between shows!
    Miss Cicely Courtneidge played the *Empire* on 17 December 1917, as
a young girl. She found great fame thirty five years later as Gay Daventry
in '*Gay's the Word*', which played the *Empire* for two weeks from 13
October 1952 after its run at the *Saville Theatre*, London. Her husband,
Jack Hulbert, put the idea to Ivor Novello who wrote this, his last show,
with lyrics by Alan Melville. Thorley Walters and Lizabeth Webb co-

starred. its now famous songs included '*If Only He'd Looked My Way*', and '*On Such a Night as This*'.

Mr Robb Wilton (1881-1957), appeared on 13 May 1918. His real name was Smith. He had a stage career spanning fifty nine years. In later years his top of the bill sketches were '*The Magistrate*' and '*The Fire Station*, partnered by his wife Florence Palmer. He had a long list of lugubrious monologues; as Miss Evelyn Laye sang from 'Phil the Fluter' 'They don't make them like that anymore'. On Monday 12 December 1938, he presented '*Mr Muddlecome at Home*'. His most famous line was '*The day war broke out, my Missus said to me ...*'.

Mr Will Hay (1888-1949) appeared on 3 March 1919. Having spent the early days of his career touring with the Fred Karno company of comedians from 1909, he is best remembered for the film '*Oh! Mr Porter*'.

Mr Jack Buchanan played the *Empire* during the week commencing 14 February 1921. Some years later he played 'Buttons', for the first time, in '*Cinderella*', with Adele Dixon and Fred Emney. He tried to teach one of the leading ladies a simple dance step which although easy, she could not pick up. The show opened on the 24 December 1940. On Monday 9 June 1941, he also appeared in a comedy thriller '*The Body Was Well Nourished*', with Elsie Randolph.

The star attraction at the *Empire* on Friday 20 July 1923, at 2.30pm was presented to the audience with great pride by managers, Mr Donald Arthur and Mr Edmund Russon. The attraction being none other than the great Anna Pavlova. Supported by Laurent Novikoff and Hilda Butsova, the celebrated Russian ballet stars, she presented a programme of Egyptian Dances, Serenade, Bachanale and her famous '*The Swan*'. (Choreographie by Saint Saens). She returned to the Theatre in 1930, for one week, commencing on Monday 10 November, for one week with a complete change of programme from the Thursday. Supporting company for the world famous Pavlova included Pierre Vladimiroff and a full Corps de Ballet. Performances were once nightly at 7.30pm. The programme included, Monday to Wednesday '*Polish Wedding*', '*Invitation to the Dance*', '*Russian Dance*' and a choreographic poem '*Autumn Leaves*', by Madame Pavlova who portrayed a chrysanthemum, to the music of Chopin. One of her distinct triumphs. The programme from Thursday to Saturday was '*The Grotto of Venus*', with music by Tannhauser and the celebrated '*Amarilla*', one of the wonderful artiste Pavlova's greatest creations. Additional music by Glazunnoff and Drigo and a number of divertissements completed the programme. The active entertainment was superlatively delightful and Pavlova embodied the very spirit of the dance with her unparalleled skill

Empire usherettes photographed in 1939, Leah Page is second from the left,

as an interpreter. At a reputed forty nine years old, though actually fifty (1881-1931), she still retained the brilliance of her art and skill. A Russian exile, she still declared it to be the most wonderful country in the world, full of poetry and music. Always concluding '*I should love to return...but...*' All the pathos lay in her unfinished sentence. A year later, the seemingly immortal Pavlova was dead! However, the world was changing and ironically the swastika relief edging on the Pavlova show reviews in the *Yorkshire Telegraph* and *Star* was an omen of things to come.

Mrs Iris Gibson recalls that her mother, Mrs Leah Croft (then Miss Page), was a Tiller Girl at this time and sat in the balcony at the *Empire* to see the first programme on Wednesday 12 November. After the performance, the great ballerina was resting but Leah Page waited outside the stage door for her to come out. It was a bitterly cold night and her efforts were rewarded when Madame Pavolva gave her a lily of the valley flower from her bouquet. Today, what remains of this magical moment is a programme photograph and the faded remnants of this pressed lily, after nearly seventy years! Mrs Gibson has generously donated these to the author, who was delighted to accept such a treasured momento of a starstruck Pavlova fan's moment of glory. Mrs Croft became an usherette at the *Empire Theatre*, between 1936 and 1940. Mrs Gibson followed in her mother's footsteps. As a young girl she danced in pantomimes at the *Empire* and *Lyceum* theatres). The ballet was always popular with *Empire* audiences and from 28 August 1950, Julian Braunsweg presented 'Gala Performances', of Ballet with Anton Dolin, Natalie Kraswswovska, a full corps de ballet and symphony orchestra. The programme included '*Petrouchka*', '*Swan Lake Act Two*', '*The Nutcracker*' and '*Les Sylphides*'.

Miss Gracie Fields (real name Grace Stansfield, 1898-1979) played the *Empire* on 7 January 1924, in '*Mr Tower of London*'. Following a provincial tour, the show played the *Alhambra Theatre*, Leicester Square, London. This theatre was demolished in 1936 and the site is now occupied by the *Odeon Cinema*. Her appearance at the *Alhambra*, made her a star overnight. In some 3,000 performances over a five year period, no cast member failed to play. The charming Gracie well deserved the title 'Queen of Revue'. The company included her sisters, Edith and Betty and brother Tommy Fields. This clever concoction of comic episodes had abundant humour, talent and brightness. Written by Gracie's then husband, Archie Pitt, who also played the leading male role. Archie also presented Gracie, Edith and Tommy Fields in a new revue '*By Request*'. From 26 April 1926, featuring '*The Waxworks*' and

Original 'Pavlova' programme and preserved flowers from her bouquet, 1930. Courtesy of Sheffield Newspapers Ltd.

PAVLOVA
LILY. OF. VALLEY. GIVEN. TO. LEAH. BY. PAVLOVA. EMPIRE. STAGE. DOOR. ON. 12ᵗ NOVEMBER · 1930.

'*In Hospital*'. Many years later in 1947, during the week commencing 26 May, Tommy Fields, appeared in variety with Du Marte and Denzar, '*Flying Skeletons Alive*'. A backcloth with luminous paint and ultra violet light completed the presentation. Miss Fields also appeared again at the *Empire* on Monday 8 March 1929, in a New Musical Production '*The Show's The Thing*'.

Fred Karno's 'Revels', presented '*Miss 1925*' from 6 April 1925, with Doris Ashton and Harry Herbert.

Francis Laidler presented a superlative revue starring Miss Gwladys Stanley (his later wife) '*The Roundabout*', during the week commencing 25 May 1925. Miss Stanley was a very popular revue artist and appeared with the star comedian Tom D. Newell. John Tillers London *Palace* girls appeared and twenty strikingly effective scenes were executed by Captain Oliver P Bernard. The brilliant costumes were designed by Miss Dolly Tree and Princess Andrew, of Russia. It was a whirl of mirth and melody. Since the revue ran for over two hours, the curtain up time was altered to 6.20pm and 8.40pm. This record breaking *Empire* show returned by public demand on 10 August 1925.

Gwladys Stanley also appeared from 22 October 1928, in the Julian Wylie production '*Blackpool Follies of 1928*'. This came direct from the *Winter Gardens Theatre*, Blackpool and was in seventeen episodes with twenty six scenes! Set in Blackpool itself, the show included, 'Marks and Spencers', 'The Tower Circus' and the 'Empress Ballroom'. Co-stars were Naughton and Gold, (Charles John Naughton, 1887-76 and James McGonigal, 1886-1967). Bertram Rodgers, and a company of seventy five artists, including twenty four 'baby belles'.

A favourite at the *Empire* was Wee Georgie Wood, real name George Balmer (1897-1979), who played there in the week commencing 22 November 1926. He made further appearances from 22 April 1940 in variety with Dolly Harmer in a '*Mrs Robinson and Her Son*' episode. On Monday 2 December and in '*Madhatters of 1940*', on Monday 26 July 1948. George was often described as the 'Peter Pan of the Halls'. He worked with his stage Mother, Dolly Harmer, until she passed away in 1956.

The 'Cheekie Chappie', Mr Max Miller, his real name was Thomas Henry Sargeant, (1894-1963), was a rare visitor to Sheffield. His trademarks were flamboyant suits in outrageous floral patterns with plus fours, kipper tie and a jauntily angled white Homburg. The risque stories which the audience were asked to choose from his 'White or Blue?', books, and his signature tune '*Mary from the Dairy*', took him to the top of his profession. His explosive Cockney humour and comic skills enabled him to hold audiences in the palm of his hand. This great 'front of cloth', comic played the *Empire* on 29 November 1926, 23 October 1933 and when his career was waning, on 28 February 1955. He was the pure gold of Music Hall loved by women and envied by men. In his own words, 'Miller's the name lady – there'll never be another.' He was truly unique

The *Empire Theatre* closed on 20 June 1927 for alterations and general redecoration. After a ten week refurbishment, the theatre reopened.

Mr Bobby Howes and Miss Binnie Hale, appeared in the musical comedy '*Mr Cinders*' on 19 November 1928. Arthur Lucan, (real name Towle; 1887-1954), whose opening line was '*Good evening blackguards, bodyguards and fire guards*', played the *Empire Theatre* many times with Kitty McShane born 1897, in his famous sketch '*Old Mother Riley and her Daughter Kitty*'. (His first stage name was Mrs O'Flynn). Old Mother Riley was always sitting by the dying fire in the cottage hearth waiting for the late returning daughter Kitty from a night out with Danny Boy. Looking at her watch and muttering the immortal lines '*its tomorrow today*' with much manic hand waving. Husband and wife, their act often reflected their off stage life. A keen business woman, she handled the shows as 'Kitty McShane Productions' and controlled their financial affairs, public knowledge of which made their sketches an even bigger draw. Unpopular with her husband and cast, she regarded them all with contempt. It was not uncommon to hear them arguing loudly in their dressing room at the *Empire* before and after the show. They split up in 1951 and Arthur carried on the act with a new partner. His last film appearance was in '*Old Mother Riley Meets the Vampire*', co-starring with Bela Lugosi in 1952.

Arthur Lucan's genius died suddenly on stage, at the *Hull Tivoli Theatre* on 17 May 1954. His neglected grave in a Hull churchyard was renovated by the late 'camp' comedian, Larry Grayson. Lucan's act continued in later years with his understudy, the late Roy Roland taking his part, until Miss McShane died in 1964, after which the act, which had remained as an exact carbon copy of the original, disappeared from the stage until 1973, when it was revived by Roy Roland and Danny La Rue as '*Kitty*' at the *Opera House*, Blackpool.

Lucan and McShane played the *Empire* on 27 May 1929, Monday 28 October 1940. '*Old Mother Riley Pays us a Visit*' played on Monday 17 April 1944 and Monday 28 May 1945. An entirely new production appeared on Monday 28 October 1946.

Around this time death struck on the *Empire* stage. Franzoni Attilio, aged 43, from Bologna, Italy was appearing on a variety bill. Strong man of the 'Apollo Trio', he collapsed during the act and the curtain was rung down. The doctor pronounced him life extinct. The cause as reported by the stage manager Mr Herbert Parsons, being tremendous weight on his chest muscles affecting his heart.

Miss Hylda Baker, (1908-86), was a firm favourite with *Empire* audiences and appeared on 3 June 1929. Later appearances include from 1 October 1945, billed as the 'comedy girl'. She was a down to earth, dumpy know all character with a pure and simple vulgarity, without any offence in it. Her famous act with its Lancashire accent and slant, featured a very tall thin man in female attire as the 'stooge' called 'Cynthia'. Hylda's favourite catch phrase over the years was '*She knows y' know*', which also became her show's title. Her *Empire* presentation on Monday 30 April 1956. Over the years that followed there were other catch phrases, the most memorable of which were, '*I must get a little hand put on this watch*' and '*Have you been?*'. This tiny character dressed in a loud check suit with floppy hat and bit of rabbit fur was greatly loved by Sheffield audiences. She spewed malapropisms with amazing rapidity. Great fame came to Miss Baker with her appearances on television in the 1970s in '*Nearest and Dearest*', co-starring Jimmy Jewel. Jimmy's first stage appearance was at the tender age of five. He was shot up through the stage trapdoor as a 'demon' breaking his shoulder!

During February and March 1999, Miss Jean Fergusson, of '*Last of the Summer Wine*' fame, toured the country with her one woman show about Hylda Baker. This superb personification was made all the more realistic by the use of a large set built to scale, which created for the audience, the illusion of her being similar in stature to Miss Baker. Set in a dressing room, this excellent production traced Hylda Baker's often traumatic life story from fame and fortune to suffering from Alzheimer's disease. Her lifes dread then was to lose her memory, so vital to any performer. When she died, she was completely alone. Miss Fergusson's brilliant presentation was an accurate and compelling portrayal of triumph and disaster.

The tremendous musical '*Showboat*', sailed into the *Empire Theatre*

The author pictured with Miss Jean Fergusson, during her apperance in the pantomine 'Jack and the Beanstalk', 1998.

on Monday 18 February 1929, for a three week season. Performances were once nightly, with matinees on Thursday and Saturday at 2.30pm. This was the latest sensation from the *Theatre Royal*, Drury Lane, London and was an immediate success. The stupendous production consisted of fifteen scenes with a company of 110 artistes, including 31 principals and two complete choruses. Mr William Senior played 'Gaylord Ravanel' and Mr Gilbert Holland 'Joe', in which part he sang '*Ole Man River*', with both plaintive and dramatic effect. This triumph of musical theatre had hauntingly tuneful melodies, tense drama and bright comedy allied to acting and dancing of an exemplary standard.

In October 1929 another show direct from Drury Lane arrived at the *Empire*. On this occasion, Messrs MacDonald and Young presented the romance of the Canadian Rockies, '*Rose Marie*'. This show was in nine scenes and featured Mr Arthur Rees as 'Sergeant Malone', the Mountie and Miss Lennie Deane in the title role. They performed the '*Indian Love Call*', to great effect and the rousing chorus of Indians sang '*Totem Tom Tom*' with enthusiasm. At this time the theatre produced a free magazine entitled the *Empire Tatler*. An excellent three course theatre dinner could also be had from 6.00pm, by arrangement with Davy's Victoria Cafe, Fargate, for the modest outlay of 3/6. (17.5p!). The old Davy's site is now occupied by W.H. Smith Ltd. A parking station was also provided for motor cars in the nearby Charles Street and a uniformed attendant took charge of patrons cars. Undercover parking was also available on the premises of Messrs Brook Shaws, opposite the main theatre entrance. Apart from including information on parking and forthcoming attractions, the magazine included such snippets of advice as asking ladies to remove their hats and requesting physicians to acquaint the Box Office with their seat numbers.

Croft House Amateur Operatic Society moved from the *Lyceum* to the *Empire* in 1930 and on 3 February presented '*The Gay Parisienne*', by Offenbach. Miss Zena Dare appeared at the theatre on 10 February in '*The First Mrs Fraser*', wearing a series of elegant gowns as she played the title role. On 7 April, Ivor Novello presented '*Symphony in Two Flats*', and from Monday 28 April, Miss Mona Vivien appeared in '*Funny Side Up*', a new review presented by Bert Montague.

The week commencing Tuesday 7 October saw the staging of the famous 'Co-Optimists', starring Mr Stanley Holloway(real name Stanley Augustus Holloway, 1890-1982) and Mr Billy Mayerl. This was another successful show from London, the reputation of which was maintained in the provinces. Mr Stanley Holloway was billed as '*A voice and some mimicry*' and won a well deserved encore for his presentation of '*The Volga Boatman*'. He also brought the house down with '*Waterloo*', while his impersonations of Maurice Chevalier and Challiapine were brilliantly funny. Mr Billy Mayerl, a pianist of considerable talent, played an aire simultaneously on two pianos.

Stanley Holloway appeared again at the *Empire* on Monday 22 June 1936, in '*Lancashire Delights*'. In a welcome change from revue, this stage, screen and radio star headed an attractive variety bill. Wearing a scarf, cap, or bowler hat, he delighted the audience with such monologues as, Albert Ramsbottom and his unfortunate experience with a lion, or Samuel Small's Medal and 'Brahn Boots!' He also regaled his audience with the tale of how Yorkshire Pudding came into existence. His artistry denoted the versatility necessary from a burlesque artist. Supporting artists were 'The Four Jokers', clever acrobatic dancers and Edward Victor, 'A remarkable Shadowgraphist', who created life like pictures of notable persons from shadows cast by his hands.

Stanley Holloway later found immortal fame in the stage and screen role of Alfred P. Doolittle, a common dustman, in the stage musical '*My Fair Lady*' with Julie Andrews and the 1964 film with Rex Harrison and Audrey Hepburn.

From Monday 13 October 1930 the presentation was 'Rio Rita', set in sunny Mexico. The leading parts being played by Mr Howett Morster, Mr Freddie Forbes and Miss Daisy Elliston.

The week commencing 1 February 1932 saw the world famous D'Oyly Carte Opera Company in their one and only visit to the *Empire*. Mr Rupert D'Oyly Carte presented their strongest company ever to go on tour including, Sir Henry Litton, Sydney Granville, Martyn Green, Darrell Fancourt, Rita Mackay and recently returned from Australia, Dorothy Gill. There was a powerful chorus and a large augmented orchestra under the baton of Isidore Godfrey. Performances were once nightly at 7.30pm with a feast of musical fare to suit all tastes. The programme for the week ran as follows: Monday, '*The Mikado*', Tuesday, '*The Gondoliers*', Wednesday, '*Ruddigore*', Thursday, Matinee '*The Mikado*', evening, '*The Yeoman of the Guard*', Friday, '*Iolanthe*' and Saturday, '*The Gondoliers*'. Both the *Mikado* and *Gondoliers*, were lavish and highly spectacular productions with new costumes and scenery designed by Mr Charles Ricketts RA. The company was composed entirely of British artists. Mr Gilbert and Mr Sullivan offered their audiences delicious entertainment in these operatic gems. Their magical partnership which lasted 25 years echoed through the Victorian era. Gilbert's piercing comic observations, often political, made theatre history and Sullivan's operetta compositions overshadowed his traditional concert work. The original '*Mikado*' opened in London during the Japanese exhibition of 1885.

All seats were bookable and the theatre was regularly crowded, an infrequent scene in those days.

From Monday 7 February 1932, Croft House Amateur Operatic Society presented their third show at the *Empire*, 'The Girls of Gottenburg', once nightly at 7.30pm and a Saturday Matinee at 2.00pm. Special prices from 1/- to 5/9 were available. This was a lavish production with tuneful songs, rousing choruses, pretty dresses and spectacular scenery. This excellent entertainment readily demonstrated what an amateur group can produce, given adequate facilities.

The orchestra was under Mr Desmond MacMahon and several old favourites among the cast included, Cecil Everitt, T. Alec Seed, Bert Peacock, Mrs C. Everitt, Miss Doris Sadler and Mr W.B. Greaves. (In 1931 they had presented 'Princess Charming').

In 1939 the Society presented its finest in a long line of successful shows. This was Ivor Novello's 'Glamorous Night', and was magnificently mounted with extraordinarily effective costumes and sets. Maurice Hampton took the Novello role of Anthony Allen and clearly revelled in his task, while Olivia Turner presented a fine acting and singing talent as 'Militza'. She left her sick bed to appear on the first night. Sheffield theatre-goers turned out in their thousands to see this refreshing and unspoiled production, which was directed by Laurie Lingard.

Croft House Society presented several other musicals at the *Empire* over the years, including Noel Coward's musical play, 'Bitter Sweet', on 26 February 1946, the score of which included 'I'll see you again' and 'Ladies of the Town'. During the week commencing Monday 3 March 1952, they presented their Jubilee Presentation 'The Lisbon Story', with John Bonner, Laurie Lingard and Myra Cooper as 'Gay Girard'. Programmes for this event were priced at 3d. (1.5p in decimal currency).

From 15 February 1932, Carl Brisson appeared at the *Empire* in 'The Merry Widow'. This was an enormous attraction being the greatest of all musical comedies. The large company included Miss Helen Gilliland and Mr George Graves.

From 6 June 1932, Billy Cotton and his band appeared with the vocalists Alan Breeze and Dolly Elsie. A supporting artist was Dick Henderson, 'The Yorkshire Nightingale and comedian'(1891-1958). This was the father of the late Dickie Henderson (real name Richard Matthew Henderson 1922-85). Henderson senior was a fat little man whose signature tune was 'Tiptoe Through the Tulips' and his trademarks were a tiny bowler hat and a thick lighted cigar. Also on the bill were 'Duncans Collies - Canine Actors', Alma Victoria, 'The Girl on Wheels' and Valentine - Vaudevilles Slickest Cartoonist'.

Mr Sandy Powell, born in Rotherham, 'Can you hear me mother?'

On Monday 25 July 1932, for one week only, Mr Harry Tate Junior appeared at the theatre in his famous sketch *'Golfing'*. This bill also included 'Mr George Hirste - The Dame Character' and 'Marie Lawton and her Harp'.

From 30 December 1932, seasonal entertainment was provided by The Royal Italian Circus, and *Empire* patrons had the opportunity to see a complete staged circus performance complete with elephants, ponies, dogs, monkeys, acrobats, jugglers, trapeze artists and world famous clowns. Also Mr Eugene Sandow (born in Prussia 1867), who last appeared in Sheffield as 'Samson', *'the strongest man on Earth'*, whose act included tearing telephone directories in half.

The week commencing Monday 4 March 1946 also saw the presentation of *'The Mammoth Circus'*, by Tom Arnold for Albion Operas Ltd. Besides horses, lions and seals, there also appeared, the world's most famous musical clowns, 'The Cairoli Brothers'.

Mr Clarkson Rose (1890 - 1968), appeared with Sandy Powell on 26 October 1931, in the revue *'Carnival Time'* presented by Harry Norris. Rose also played the *Empire* on Monay 18 March 1946, on a variety bill with Henry Hall's Orchestra. From 6 September 1937, Sandy Powell appeared in one of his many 'Road Shows' with Kenneth Cooper, the fifteen year old syncopation genius. Billed as *'The Famous Stage, Radio, Screen and Gramophone Star'*, he appeared on Monday 27 February 1939 and in 1940 with 'The Damie Beach Lovelies' and 'Ernest Shannon, Ace Impressionist'. Rotherham born and bred, in 1900 Sandy Powell began his stage career in local clubs, working with his Mother as 'Lilly and Sandy'. He never topped the bill on the number one *Empire* circuit. His famous catchphrase was *'Can you hear me Mother?'* He died in 1982 and was the last of the Burlesque performers.

From 3 July 1933, the *Empire* closed for redecoration, lighting and structural alterations, which included the installation of a new Bioscope box in the roof.

From 23 October, the sisters, Misses Elsie and Doris Waters, played the theatre as 'Gert and Daisy' and also in radio variety on Monday 22 November 1937, with 'Monsewer' Eddie Grey, (Edward Earl Grey. 1898

- 1969), and Mr Billy Danvers. Their famous brother, Mr Jack Warner, played the *Empire* from 3 February 1941, for two weeks in '*Garrison Theatre*', presented by Jack Hylton, courtesy of the BBC. A supporting act was George Moon and Burton Brown, New Radio Team. Jack Warner later found fame as a policeman in BBC television's '*Dixon of Dock Green*'.

On Saturday 18 November 1933, there was a charity matinee in aid of the poor children's seaside fund, presented by the Constance Grant Academy of Dancing 'Dance Revuette'.

In 1932 Miss Patricia Dawson had appeared in their similar presentation, aged five, singing '*So Shy*', while performing a dance routine. Her costume was created by Miss Grant's mother, a professional dressmaker. It consisted of a bright red georgette blouse with silver steel lame trousers, red satin tap shoes and a floppy brimmed silver and red hat. She also appeared in the following year's production.

Mr Louis Armstrong made an appearance at the *Empire*, on 26 March 1934.

Flanagan and Allen of '*Underneath the Arches*', fame played the *Empire* on 17 September 1934. They originally teamed up at the Mansfield *Empire Theatre* and the Irish name Bud Flanagan, was suggested to them by Miss Florrie Ford when Chesney Allen was her road manager. A good name for a Cockney Jew! (real name Reuben Weintrop, 1896-1988)

From 9 September 1935, Mr Hughie Green and his Gang appeared. At the time he was a fifteen year old, being the youngest broadcaster, actor and producer in England. The gang were all children of a similar age. Supporting acts included 'Senator Murphy, the Political Humorist' and 'Ray Huling and Charlie' an amazing seal who 'danced' the hula hula in a grass skirt! Hughie Green found fame with the radio show, '*In Town Tonight*' and later on

Miss Pat Dawson, Empire 1932.

Mr Ramon Novarro

television in '*Double your Money*' and '*Opportunity Knocks*'.

On Monday 15 November 1937, Prince Littler presented '*The Frog*', a mystery play from the novel by Edgar Wallace.

The week commencing Monday, 3 March 1936 saw a personal appearance in a variety bill of Mr Ramon Novarro, at that time, screenlands most romantic figure. On Monday 14 April, the evergreen musical comedy '*The Merry Widow*' was again presented with Mr Jay Laurier and Miss Nita Croft. The show was beautifully staged and dressed with an excellent chorus. Miss Croft also appeared in '*White Horse Inn*', for three weeks commencing 30 November 1948 and this very popular musical returned on 29 November for three more weeks in 1949.

Mr Ben Lyon and Miss Bebe Daniels appeared on 21 March 1938, and Mr Tommy Handley presented '*The Dis-Orderly Room*', on Monday 4 April. Miss Evelyn Laye played the *Empire* from 15 August 1938 and also for two weeks from 26 September 1955 in '*Wedding in Paris*' with Barry Sinclair.

The week commencing Monday 18 September 1938, saw Mr George Formby, real name George Hoy Booth, (1904 - 1961), appearing in variety with his wife Beryl in '*The Casting Office*' and also '*With his Uke*'.

Mr Albert Modley was always top of the bill when he appeared at the *Empire* and a firm favourite with patrons. 'Lancashire's favourite Yorkshire Comedian', appeared from 7 November 1938, with '*On With The Modley*' and with the same titled show from 15 March 1948, for two weeks. A feature was Mr Jimmy Currie's '*Waterfalls of Scotland*', including the Highland Pipers and Dancers. He appeared in variety from 2 June 1941 with the Tiller Girls, Mildred Hammond - Soprano and Percy Garside - 'The Popular Yorkshire Baritone'. Programme price for this show was 2d.

The 1946/7 Christmas pantomime was '*Mother Goose*', again with Albert Modley, this time accompanied by Hy Hazel. Albert was to appear in the very last presentation at the *Empire* and in later years was made a Freeman of Morecambe Borough.

Miss Vera Lynn (real name Welch, born 1917) appeared in the week commencing Monday 12 December 1938. She would soon carve out a place for herself as the 'Forces' Sweetheart', immortalising the morale boosting songs '*We'll Meet Again*' and '*White Cliffs of Dover*'. In later years she was made a Dame of the British Empire and enjoyed further television success.

Miss Jessie Matthews appeared with Sonnie Hale, her then husband, for two weeks commencing 23 January 1939 in a new musical comedy,

'*I Can Take It*'. From Monday 5 February 1940, they again appeared at the *Empire* in '*Come Out To Play*', a new song, dance and comedy show. The cast included Mr Robert Dorning and Miss Matthews' gowns were by Mr Norman Hartnell. Programmes at this time were fronted with a ribbon tied cornucopia with flowers, ballerina and floral display atop!

Mr Albert Wheelan (1875-1962) the Australian entertainer and popular Broadcaster, appeared at the *Empire* from 14 August 1939, in '*A Bill of Famous Stars*'. He was the first man to have a signature tune 'The Three Brothers Waltz'. The bill included including Miss Alice Lloyd and Miss Lily Morris. As part of the show, Mr Charles Austin portrayed his well known character 'The Little Old Lady'. He also played in variety at the theatre from 19 February 1940 with 'The Dancing Dudes and Rita', Toni Borello and Mimi in 'Thrills on the Trapeze' and Henry Hall.

From 5 September 1938, Miss Helen Ford and Mr Leslie Hatton appeared in '*Please Teacher*', while the week commencing Monday 12 September 1938 saw the presentation of the original Hollywood Star Doubles, in '*Hollywood on Parade*'. When a similar show was presented from 18 December 1955, Mr Ronnie Carrol appeared in blackface in an impression of Mr Nat 'King' Cole. Ronnie's later visits to the *Empire* were as top of the bill. (He was once married to Miss Millicent Martin).

From 19 September 1938, there was a strong variety bill at the theatre, which included two firm favourites, Mr George Formby and once again, Miss Florrie Ford, who still retained her power to attract, while her old and much loved songs earned well deserved applause. Returning to Sheffield after a three year absence, George was screamingly funny in a sketch when assisted by his wife Beryl. Needless to say, he also earned much applause for his playing of the ukele. Supporting acts in this show were, 'The Arnaut Brothers', musical clowns and old favourites at the *Empire* and 'Red Fred', unicyclist with pep!

On 17 October 1938, Jack Taylor's new review '*King Revel*' opened. This featured Mr Billy Russell, '*On Behalf of the Working Man*', '*Fountains*' and '*The Tornado*', with a lady called Carina, playing the hut , while Vadio, Hertz and Mr James Rallis played the jungle and a monkey! Though Mr George Doonan also appeared in the show, what part he played is not recorded.

The first ever ice ballet to be presented in Sheffield was at the *Empire* from 24 October 1938, for two weeks, this was Tom Arnolds' '*Switzerland*'. This thrilling show was a unique theatrical experience for Sheffield patrons, with the cast using 1200 square feet of ice. The show starred Mr Albert Enders and Miss Sadie Cambridge, six times world professional ice skating champions. The second act cabaret show which featured Mr Harry Torrani, a Swiss yodeller, dispelled any possibility of monotony for the audience. Novel extravaganzas of this kind, with their graceful movements, proved to be hugely popular and several similar shows followed on from this one.

On 24 November 1953, for three weeks the show '*Chu Chin Chow*' on ice opened. This was a truly spectacular show with a cast of over 100 skaters. The leads were played by skating champions Miss Sheila Hamilton and Mr Ronald Priestly, supported by 'The Five La Founs', billed as the 'Acrobatic Cyclone' and Mr Tony Somers as 'Ali Baba'.

Direct from its success at the *Empire Pool*, Wembly and once more presented by Mr Tom Arnold, came '*The Dancing Years*', which opened on 15 March 1955. Although the production was pretty and melodious, it was not slick or sophisticated, being warm entertainment transferred to ice. There was however, something attractive about the sentimentality of the gently nostalgic melodies which were synchronised with the movement dubbed in a masterly fashion. The principal skaters were Miss Anne Rodgers, Miss Margo McMenemy Mr Leslie Lyndon. The singers were Miss Sally Anderson, Mr John Hassal and Miss Olive Gilbert. The period costumes were sumptuous and colourful and the comedy scenes were performed with an air of gay abandon by the 'Grassauer Tyrolean Boys' and 'The Harvards'.

From Monday 4 July 1955, Claude Langdon and Robert Luff presented Erik Charell's '*White Horse Inn on Ice*', for two weeks direct from the *Empress Hall*, London. Prices, including entertainment tax!, were - Stalls and Circle 10/6, Balcony 3/-.

20 March 1939 saw a Boy Scouts gang show presented by Ralph Reader and called '*Shorts 1939*'. The cast consisted of Boy Scouts from all over the city, including Mr J. Gorden Hoyes of the Beachfield troop, who still recalls the show. It was a first class song and dance show with the cubs dressed as girls performing fancy dance steps and tap dancing. The show was very well received by the *Empire*'s patrons.

For one week commencing 12 February 1940, Gilbert Miller and Jack Buchanan presented a play by Clare Booth, '*The Women*', with a cast of forty women. The show was described as '*A gorgeous castigation of the female species*'.

The Queen of Striptease, Miss Phyllis Dixey appeared at the *Empire* from 26 February 1940, in a revue presented by Charles Tucker, entitled '*Eve takes a Bow*'. This was a twice nightly show and featured Miss Dixey with her husband, Mr Jack 'Snuffy' Tracey who she had married in 1937, in a piece entitled '*The Doctors Dilemma*' (originally they toured together in '*The Sap and The Swell Dame*'). The show also featured her renowned '*The Confessions of a Fan Dancer*', which she performed using two large ostrich feather fans. For many years she held sway as Queen of this art. A 'ladylike' lady whose promised sexual thrill never materialised. Her undoubted talent was again demonstrated at the *Empire*, with the show '*Peek a Boo*', in which she was partnered by Mr Bill Kerr. The show dates were from 1 June 1946, 18 September 1950 and finally in March 1956. By the time of the 1956 appearance, Miss Dixie's career was waning, with the usual chorus of scantily clad girls reduced to only four. With the exception of radio star Gary Miller, who saved the show with his popular ballads, the rest of the cast made little impression on the *Empire*'s audience.

Mr Nat Jackley (1909-88)

From 4 March 1940, Mr Nat 'Legs' Jackley (real name Nathanial Jackley Hirsch) appeared in '*Roll out the Barrel*', a crazy revue with Jack Clifford and Eddie (Monsewer) Grey. Sketches featured Nat as a policeman in '*Flying Squad*' and as a lad in '*On The Lido*'.

From 30 September 1940 he appeared with Jack Clifford, appeared in '*Go to It*', with Harold Ramsey and his lovely ladies on the 'Mighty Theatre Organ'.

In the week commencing 2 April 1945, Nat Jackley again appeared in Tom Arnold's '*We'll be Seeing You*', a dazzling show sprinkled with established and rising stars including, Mr Ted Ray, (Charles Olden 1906-77). Ted Ray appeared again from 15 October 1945 in '*Youth Marches On*', with Miss Adelaide Hall (1901-93).

Renowned, some would say notorious, for his violin playing, Ted Ray (1906-77) presented the sketch '*Fiddlin and Foolin*'. Ted had previously presented this sketch at the *Empire* in George Black's '*Gangway*', which played from 29 May 1944 for two weeks. '*Gangway*' was staged by Robert Nesbitt, with the Wendy Toye Dancers and Miss Jill Manners. Mr Leslie A Hutchinson, 'Hutch', (1900-1969) was the first black artiste to be accepted by society. This British West Indian radio star also appeared on the bill. He appeared at the theatre again with Jimmy O'Dea in variety during 1947.

From 22 April 1940 and again from 6 April 1942,

James Jewel, father of Jimmy.

Mr Joe Loss and his big band appeared at the *Empire*.

Mr Jimmy Jewel (real name James Marsh, 1906-95) and Mr Ben Warris (1909-93) appeared many times on variety bills at the *Empire*. Sheffield born cousins, they formed a double act at the age of 25, which lasted until 1967. Their famous sketch '*Timber*', featured the pair as tree fellers. Somehow the tree always fell on Ben Warris! They played the *Empire* from 18 March 1940 and again from 23 September that year. Later they played the *Empire* on numerous occasions including, 9 April 1945, in which they featured their sketch '*Carry on 'Arry*', with Florence Desmond in support. 19 April 1948 in '*Up the Pole*', featuring twin bedlam skits brought over from their radio show and incorporating support from Percy (real name Percy Harry Thompson, 1874-1953, concertina player) and Mary Honri in '*A Concert in A Turn*'. From 24 October 1949 in '*Fate*', with a supporting act of Victor Julian and his pets. For two weeks, commencing Monday 9 July 1951, they starred in Mr Val Parnell's gay musical, '*Starlight Roof*', with Jimmy Jewel in the sketch '*Strip Tease Honeymoon*' and the pair of them in '*Here Comes the Bridegroom*'. Supporting artiste Miss Faye Lenor. From 13 April 1959, they played the *Empire* in its final year, in George and Alfred Black's revue '*Top of the Town*'. Their sketch was '*Line Engaged*', with their solo spot called '*Keep 'em Laughing*' Supporting artistes were Miss Jill Day, (Yvonne Page 1930-90) the glamorous television singing star and the famous Mr John Tiller's Girls in '*Clowns in Clover*', '*Diamond Bracelet*' and '*Stepping High*'.

More of the Tiller Girls later.

From 25 March 1940, the famous wartime radio show *ITMA* (its that man again), played in a specially adapted version for the stage. Starring

Mr Tommy Handley (1894 - 1949), billed as '*Well I'll be buttoned up - I'm back in Sheffield*'. Supporting artistes were 'Fee Fi Fo Funf' in person! Twelve most irregular 'Twittering Twerplets', from the Terps office, 'Mrs Tickle Fusspot' and Mr Maurice Denham - 'Whizz Me Past the Women's Place'. In later years Maurice Denham became a respected stage and film actor, memorably portraying the Rector in the film of D.H. Lawrence's book, '*The Virgin and the Gypsy*'.

From 29 April, 1940 for two weeks, Mr George Black presented an intimate rag '*Black Velvet*', playing simultaneously with the *Hippodrome Theatre*, London. Supporting the star, Miss Noele Gordon (later of television's *Crossroads* fame), were Miss Jill Manners, Miss Joy Hayden and in a sketch '*Come and Meet the Stars at the*

Tommy Handley
(1894-1949).

Cafe Royal', Miss Ada Reeve appeared as herself! She also played 'Lady Marne', in the sketch '*Breeding Will Tell*'. Decor was by Mr Joseph Carl. Owing to the magnitude of this production, the admission prices were increased and the first house commenced fifteen minutes earlier than usual at 6.10pm.

From 13 May 1940, Mr Jack Taylor presented '*Eve on Parade*', a colossal and spectacular revue starring Mr Albert Burdon (1900-81).

Sheffield audiences always looked forward to the visits of Mr Frank Randle, real name Arthur McEvoy, whose catchphrase '*Baaa...I've supped some ale toneet*' rang true with many of his audiences. His famous sketch '*The Old Hiker*' was a firm favourite. His classic line to a lady was '*By gum, I bet thar' a bit of a hot un!*'. For ten years his touring company was the famous 'Randle's Scandals'. More than once the police stopped the show on the

Frank Randle. (1901-1957)

grounds that his material was obscene. Often drunk on stage and always with a stout bottle close to hand, Frank belched and body noised his way through character parts as King of the comedians, a risque hero of the working class. He was a saucy safety valve for the socially straight laced 1940s. He was known in the business as 'The Stormy Petrel', with a difficult temper, which gave way in later years to alcoholism and violence. Even so the audiences, often helpless with laughter, worshipped him on stage. (In the BBC television show '*The Good Old Days*', produced by the great Mr Barney Colehan, Mr John Inman impersonated Frank Randle, whom the record books described as '*A Lancashire Music Hall comedian of immense vulgarity*'. He played the *Empire* on several occasions. During the week commencing Monday 4 November 1940, in '*North West Follies*', with supporting artist Sheffield's own Reginald Dixon, (1906-85) who for the first time on any stage played the super Lafleur organ, appearing direct from the *Tower Ballroom*, Blackpool. From 19 June 1944, Randle's 5th Edition of the '*Scandals*', of 1944 appeared with contributions from his '*Musical Maniacs*'. From 14 May 1945, the great laughter road show '*Randle's Scandals*', in a sketch as 'Stalin' and supported by 'The Spitfires', with Billy Grant and Miss Flo Ford, imitator of Florrie. She appeared in both shows inviting you to join in the old time choruses, including '*Hold your hand out, you naughty boy*', '*She's a Lassie from Lancashire*', '*Oh! Oh! Antonio*', '*Flanagan*' and '*Has anybody here seen Kelly?*'. Performing with her, the boys showed their paces!

'*Scandals of 1947*' from 10 March again featured Reginald Dixon.

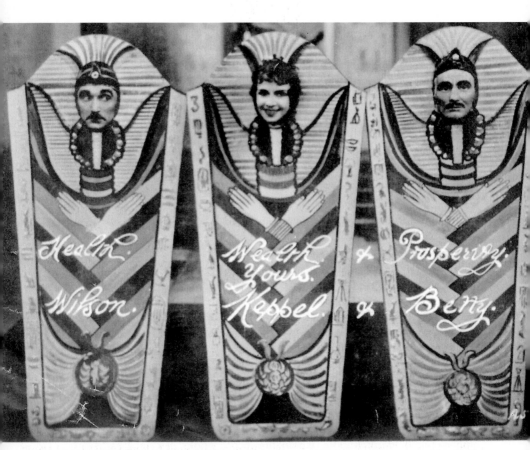

Wilson, Keppel and Betty, whose outstanding comedy was popular with artistes and audiences.

The week commencing 18 October, saw 'Scandals of 1948' with Gus Aubrey (real name Edward Brown, born 1909), female impersonator and Frank with Audrey Hewitt floundering their way through the 'Cinderella' kitchen scene as Buttons and Cinders! What a great laugh! Featuring 'The Old Hiker' and with supporting artistes, 'The Ben Abderrahman Wazzan Troupe' and Mr Stan Stafford, 'The Silver-Voiced Navvy!' From 26 September, 'Scandals of 1949', the 'new' road show featuring an additional scene 'The Old Ventriloquist', once again the 'Wazzan Troupe' and Hal Mack and his 'Dancing Demons' who would 'burn up the stage with their hot feet'. For the first time together, Jerry Allen and Rita Shearer played two Hammond Organs. The cast also included Gus Aubrey and Stan Stafford from the previous year, so not really a new show! Frank Randle was born in Wigan in 1901, his original stage name was Arthur Twist. He began his theatrical career in 1916 as an acrobat. Achieving fame in the 1930s he toured '*Randle's Scandals*' for ten years. He expressively embodied his own rather naive optimism in his performances. His health declined in the 1950s resulting in his death in Blackpool in 1957.

The celebrated comedy eccentric dance act 'Wilson Keppel and Betty', sand danced across the *Empire*'s stage from 23 September 1940 with sand scattered from Grecian urns in their sketch '*Cleopatras Nightmare*', with a supporting act from Mr Billy Bennett. In the same year they appeared with Bert Brownhill, a 'lady' of infinite laughter Joe Wilson and Jack Keppel, (born 1895), wore an ankle length white night shirt for their act, topping it off with a fez. They were thin, ancient, sombre 'Egyptians' who danced in unison to their famous 'Ballet Egyptian' Music. The original 'Betty', Betty Knox, (at one time Vaudeville partner to Jack Benny) was eventually superseded in 1941 by her daughter Patsy when the latter reached the age of 17. Over the years, there was a succession of young and attractive 'Bettys' incorporated into the act. Primarily to divert the attention of the audiences from the ever increasing age of the male members of the team.

Mr Max Wall, real name Maxwell George Lorimer, (1908-90), played the *Empire* from 18 November as 'Professor Wolovski' in '*Funny Side Up*'. He also played at the theatre with Mr Larry Adler in '*We Shall have Music*'.

During the late 1930s the storm clouds of international conflict developed with increasing menace and the *Empire* audience present on 27 September 1938, had heard Prime Minister Mr Neville Chamberlain's, 'peace in our time', speech over the radio which was relayed into the auditorium. It was followed by a burst of applause and the playing of National Anthem.

From the 8 October 1940, Mr Ivor Novello appeared for two weeks in the Drury Lane production of '*The Dancing Years*', with Miss Roma Beaumont and Miss Olive Gilbert. As he passed through the side stage curtain to conduct the orchestra, it was noted by all that he came near, that he was highly perfumed. This musical echoed the trials and tribulations of wartime life.

During the Second World War, Sheffield had one hundred and thirty air raid alerts and seventy two barrage balloons flew over the city at the time of the December 1940, blitz.

'Dear Ivor' Novello.
(1893-1951)

Blitz damage to the shop and theatre, Thursday December 12th, 1940.

From Monday 11 November 1940, Mr Lupino Lane appeared with a West End cast in the musical comedy '*Me and My Girl*', direct from 1,700 performances at the *Victoria Palace Theatre*, London. If an air raid warning was received, during wartime performances, the audience were informed from the stage. They could leave if they so desired, but the performances continued! Lupino Lane appeared in the same show again at the *Empire*, during the week commencing Monday 20 April 1959, this time in company with his son Lauri Lupino Lane (1922-86). Blokes and Donahs (cockney slang for a 'lady', originating from the Spanish word 'donna'), strutted to the 'Lambeth Walk' in the show that by this time had played over 5,000 performances in London! (New Prime Minister, Mr Winston Churchill, visited Sheffield on 8 November 1941 to view the after effects of the blitz of December 1940).

Thousands of Sheffielders pleasure bent, pursued their usual entertainment at the city's theatres. Mr Henry Hall (this is Henry Hall speaking) and his Orchestra topped the bill at the *Empire* on the night of the bombing on Thursday 12 December 1940. They played the popular hits of the day including '*Jeepers Creepers*', '*Blue Orchids*' and '*All Through a Glass of Champagne*'. The night was crisp and cold with a brilliant 'bombers moon', hanging lazily in the sky. Frost on the huddled roofs of the city reflected its nimbus of light, but soon the pavements would be frosted too with sprinkled powder of broken glass from the carnage to come.

Henry had just announced a piece of music '*Six Lessons*', which the band was playing when a tremendous explosion rocked the back of the theatre, but the band played on. Manager Mr Fred Neate, cleared the theatre audience, who emerged to the scent of smoke and brick dust hanging in the air, while fires raged in Union and Surrey Streets. Many audience members went down to the theatre boiler room and were there entertained by Henry and his band while the bombs continued to rain down outside. The *Empire* had vibrated to the orchestra and also to the drums of war. An onlooker said that the auditorium walls seemed to bow in and out at one point, such was the ferocity of the bomb blast! The city awoke from fitful and troubled sleep, to a scene of devastation. Many famous landmarks were gone, including the well known John Walsh's department store on High Street whose safe was lying among the debris. The city went through hell and the *Empire* did not escape the devastation. The theatre suffered serious damage to its

Miss Betty Driver, now of Coronation Street fame, pictured in 1942.

right dome and the shop property at the junction of Union Street and Charles Street was destroyed, along with the opposite flanking shop. Battered but unbowed, the *Empire* survived the Luftwaffe attacks, which resumed on 13 December and again on the 15 and 16 December. Henry Hall failed to turn up two days later for a Bristol radio date and a rumour swiftly spread that he had been killed in the Sheffield blitz. However he eventually turned up. The orchestra, its arrangements disorganised by the bombing and in some cases having left their instruments behind, while others were lost in the general mayhem of the bombing. Miss Betty Driver, born 1922, now of 'Coronation Street' fame, began her career as a front vocalist with Henry Hall and his Orchestra. Monday 11 August 1941, saw the presentation of Mr John Gielgud's production of 'Dear Brutus' by J M Barrie. The cast included Misses Zena Dare and Martita Hunt and Mr Roger Livesey and John Gielgud (now Sir) himself playing Dr Dearth. This was the original star cast from the *Globe Theatre*, London, which has since been renamed the

Firefighters attempt to quell the blaze at The Empire Theatre on August 3rd, 1942. The fire completely gutted the stage area. Courtesy of Sheffield Newspapers Ltd.

Gielgud in his honour.

Mr Frank Randle appeared at the theatre again on 8 December 1941 and the famous Carl Rosa Opera Company appeared for two weeks from 18 May 1942, performing '*Die Fledermaus*' and also for two weeks from 15 July 1946 with '*La Tosca*' and '*Madam Butterfly*'. They appeared again in June 1947, performing '*Faust*' and '*La Boheme*'.

Disaster struck at the *Empire* again during the war, but on this occasion it was not as a result of enemy action. On Monday 3 August 1942, a fire completely gutted the stage area. The National Fire Service, under Divisional Officer C. Teather, saved the dressing rooms, carpenter's shop and scenery flats, though the latter suffered water damage. The outbreak was discovered when the stage-doorkeeper reported for duty at 9.00am, after the theatre firewatchman had gone off duty shortly before. The fire seems to have spread very quickly, but the fire safety curtain and brick built proscenium prevented it reaching the auditorium, though at one time this metal curtain was seen to bulge in the intense heat. Finding the area under the stage filled with smoke, the doorkeeper immediately called the Fire Service.

Within a few seconds of their arrival, firemen under the command of Company Officer Jeffcott were concentrating their jets of water beneath the stage. Thick smoke poured from doors and windows at the rear of the theatre and it quickly became evident that the one fire engine present would be inadequate to quell the blaze, so reinforcements were called.

Soon six engines and pumps were feverishly at work on the blaze. Flames reached scenery on the stage and promptly leapt to the roof, setting that ablaze. The stage was now an inferno. Not until great streams of water poured through the roof, from turntable ladders equipped with powerful hoses, was it possible for the firemen to gain access to the stage area, which was the seat of the blaze. Ordinarily the stage would have been clear of scenery but the settings for Mr Ernie Lotinga's new production '*The Gestapo*', were fixed on the previous day, in preparation for the Tuesday matinee. This scenery for this production, valued at £3,000, was completely destroyed. Fortunately, the theatres scenery dock and its contents were not badly damaged and the costumes for the show which were in the dressing rooms, were also saved.

Divisional Officer Teather who directed the firefighting operations said to *The Star*,

> '*The men did some excellent work especially those on the turntable escape ladders, directing water onto the roof. They stuck it despite the heat and smoke and this helped to save the dressing rooms*'.

Flying slates and sparks fell on adjoining property and a further small outbreak of fire was discovered in the roof of a nearby building, however, this was quickly dealt with and damage minimised. During the operations at the *Empire*, Company officer Jeffcott was overcome by smoke while inside the building, but managed to make his way outside, where he collapsed and was taken to the Royal Hospital. Other firemen were affected by the smoke but soon recovered sufficiently, to carry on with their task. Interviewed at the time, Mr Neate could not say whether the stage would be rebuilt during the war, but added '*On the face of it, I doubt it, owing to the government restrictions on the amount of re-building which can take place*'. At that time, repairs costing more than £100 being banned for premises not directly involved in war work. While the fire raged at the rear of the theatre, dozens of people were at the front, trying to book seats for the forthcoming matinee! There was concern that the theatre might have to remain closed until after the war, since stage rebuilding costs of several thousand pounds would far exceed the £100 spending limit imposed by the Government. However, because the blaze left Sheffield with only one operating city centre theatre, the *Lyceum*, special permission was given for repairs to be carried out. The *Empire* was closed until 6 September 1943. The fireman pictured atop the ladder , see illustration, is Mr Ron Harrison who recalls that a newly installed 'Z', battery of rocket firing anti-aircraft guns stationed at Shirecliffe, first fired on a German reconnaissance plane flying over the city whilst he was fighting the *Empire Theatre* stage blaze. However, the rocket was unable to reach the plane.

Other bands to appear at the *Empire* during the mid 1940s, were Maurice Winnick, Felix Mendleson and his 'Hawaiian Serenaders' and Billy Hind. Miss Ivy Benson (1913-93) and her all girl band appeared from 7 August 1944, with the comedian, 'Stainless Stephen', real name Arthur Clifford Baynes (1892 - 1972). His act was peppered with spoken punctuation such as comma, colon and full stop. Sheffield born, his nickname was acquired when he appeared at the *Empire*, wearing a steel waistcoat specially commissioned from Firth-Vickers, he later added a steel hat band. He also appeared during the week commencing 13 August 1951.

Miss Benson and her band also played the Theatre from the week commencing Monday 9 April 1945, with Jewel and Warriss and Miss Florence Desmond (1905-93) female impressionist, as supporting acts.

Mr Carroll Levis, (1910-1968) Britain's 'Star Maker', played the *Empire* with his BBC radio discoveries from Monday 27 June 1944. (He discovered Jim Dale, whose real name is Jim Smith). His famous signature tune was 'Stardust'.

This was also also the era of the great illusionists.

From Monday 20 November 1944, 'The Great Lyle', presented an entertainment of bewildering amazement, with among other things, a flying gramophone!, an enactment of Indian fable, and Lilyan Dickinson, 'The Cunning Bunny', who had been sawn in half 4,300 times! Mr Billy Danvers was the supporting artiste (William Mikado Danvers died 1964).

Other illusionists including, 'Dante', (known as 'Sima Sala Bim'), and 'Kalanag' also played the *Empire*, performing their magical and illusory feats.

'The Great Lyle', played the *Empire* again from Monday 30 July 1951, with his '*Mystery Box*', revue. He had previously appeared during the week commencing Monday 1 October 1945, with Miss Hylda Baker in support.

Mr Norman Evans presented, from Monday 26 November, the great laughter show for young and old, '*Good Evans*'. Supporting artistes were Ted Andrews and Barbara, respectively stepfather and mother of Miss Julie Andrews.

Norman Evans (1901 - 1962), appeared for many years at the *Empire* with his famous sketch entitled '*Over the Garden Wall*'. In this he portrayed a middle-aged Lanchashire harrridan 'Fanny Fairbottom', who was given to gossip confiding secrets to her invisible neighbour. She wore a red wig, mob cap, glasses and was missing a few molars! She used to lose her balance and bruise her ample chest on the brick wall time and time again! Needless to say, the audience loved it! Billed as 'Lancashire's Ambassador of Mirth', he played the *Empire* again during the week commencing Monday 20 October 1947 and from Monday 4 May 1953 with Miss Betty Jumel (1901-90) and the 'Twelve John Tiller Girls'.

The Tiller Girls were famous for their performances at the *Empire* and appeared many times. From Monday 16 October 1939, they appeared in '*This'll Make You Laugh*' and from Monday 13 April 1959, in '*Top of the Town*' with Jewel and Warris. Norman Evans always insisted on working with the Tillers and was described by them as a kind and caring man. He and his wife always looked after the girls. He lost an eye as a result of a car accident, which occurred whilst he was travelling to the Sunderland *Empire Theatre*, when he swerved his stretch limousine to avoid killing a cat!

From Monday 3 December 1945, Mr Bernard Delfont presented a new production of '*Rose Marie*' with Miss Cherry Lind and Mr George Moon. (From 27 August 1945, he presented the famous musical comedy '*No No Nanette*'. His wife, Miss Carol Lynne appeared at the *Empire* with Mr Arthur Clarke in '*The Student Prince*', in the week commencing Monday 30 April 1945). Bernard Delfont also presented '*The Gipsy Princess*' in December 1945.

From Monday 1 April 1946, Nat Mills and Bobbie, (Nathan Miller, 1900-93 and Bobbie McCauley who died in 1955) radio's 'Rare Pair' appeared in '*Let's Get On With It*'. They also played in variety from Monday 20 August 1943, Monday 27 August 1945 and Monday 1 September 1947.

From Monday 8 April, George and Alfred Black presented '*Hip-Hip-Hooray*', with Maurice, Joyce, Bonar and George Colleano. Miss Ann Shelton (Patricia Sibley, 1923-94) played at *The Empire* in variety in August, singing '*Lay down your arms*' (and surrender to me) and '*My Yiddisher Momma*'. And she was Catholic!

Mr Charlie Chester and Mr Arthur Haynes (died 1966) appeared in '*Stand Easy*' during the week, commencing 10 March 1947, while Deirdrie Doyle and Fanny Wright appeared from 12 May 1947 in '*Arsenic and Old Lace*'.

On the behalf of the Air Council, from 19 May, Mr Ralph Reader presented '*Wings*', the epic story of the Royal Air Force.

From Monday 26 August, Mr Michael Miles presented '*Radio Forfeits*', with the Yes! ? No! interlude, which later became '*Take Your Pick*', on BBC television. Supporting artistes were Mr George Lacy 'She's No Lady' and once again Mr Max Wall. Similary, Mr Wilfred Pickles (1904-78) invited audience member to 'Have a go'. He toured with Violet Carson (Ena Sharples of *Coronation Street*), his wife Mabel and Barney Colehan.

Monday 22 March 1948, saw Mr Albert Modley, 'Nice to be daft', who played the *Empire* in '*On With The Modley*', he was known as 'Lancashire's Favourite Yorkshire Comedian'. Mr Frankie Howard, (real name Francis Alick Howard, 1917-92) whose career blossomed after this first *Empire* performance, appeared in the week commencing 5 April 1948 and from 9 April 1951.

The exterior of The Empire in 1959, showing blitz damage to the right turret.

The week commencing Monday 12 April, saw the opening of '*The Tommy Trinder Show*', '*You lucky people!*', with the Tiller Girls in '*Beside the Seaside*'.

From 24 July, the legendary Miss Dorothy Squires (real name Edna May Squires) played the Theatre. She was of course famous for her singing of the song '*Say it with Flowers*'. She was supported on this occasion by Mr Billy Reid and '?The Solovox?'.

From Monday 25 October, there was a personal appearance of the famous film star Mr George Formby, assisted by his ever present wife Beryl and with a full variety company in support.

The week commencing Monday 4 April 1949, was the turn of Pete Collins' new show '*Would You Believe It?, The Strangest Show on Earth*', featuring 'The Mighty Mannequin', 'The Belgian Giant Atlas' and Bobby Davis who danced with tables in his teeth!

Empire Playbill, August 1951 revue with Bartlett and Ross; Ford and Sheen.

Monday 1 August introduced '*The Melody Lingers On*', with Mr Issy Bonn and during the week commencing Monday 8 August, Mr Mannie Jay and Mr Sydney Myers presented '*Soldiers in Skirts*', a laughter revue. This louche presentation featured an all male cast recently discharged from HM Forces, which played over 1800 performances and was seen by over two million people. The artistes in this en mass drag show were, according to a member of the theatre staff at the time, very proficient knitters of sweaters and scarves! This production again played the *Empire* in the week commencing 31 July 1950.

From 12 June 1950, Mr Alan Jones, the famous Hollywood singing star and father of Jack Jones, appeared with a big variety company. His renditions of '*The Donkey Serenade*' and '*Make Believe*', were much appreciated by the Sheffield audiences.

Mr Harry Secombe (1921-) appeared in variety from 26 March 1951 and Mr Max Bygraves (real name Walter, born 1922) also appeared from 25 June 1951 with Miss Joan Turner, (Joan Teresa Page 1922-) comedienne/singer with the voice of an angel - the wit of a devil.

The equally popular singer Mr Donald Peers (1910 - 1973), played the *Empire* in the week commencing 29 July 1946. This star of song performed his famous signature tune '*By a Babbling Brook*', and was supported by the BBC feature '*They're Out*'. In November 1951, he appeared at the *Empire* with Morecambe and

Empire programme, August 1946. Variety bill with G H Elliott and Miss Anne Shelton.

Wise, Billy Danvers and 'Dr Crock and his Crackpots' (real name Harry Hines, 1903-71). He played the *Empire* again in October 1957.

On Monday 1 October 1951, '*To Look at Me*', a show of fun and spectacle starring Mr Reg 'Confidentially', and 'Proper Poorley', Dixon (1915-84), arrived at the *Empire*. He also appeared with Margery Manners, in the week commencing 5 June 1950 and was famous for his part in the radio show Variety Band Box! Supporting artistes were the Alen Brothers and June. 'Two sparks and a flame!'

Week commencing 8 October, was when Mr Emile Littler, presented an entirely new production of the world famous comedy '*The Maid of the Mountains*', with Sonny Jenks and company of sixty artistes.

In the week commencing 18 June, '*Highlights of Radio*', with Semprini, (1908-90) 'Old ones, new ones, loved ones, neglected ones'. He also appeared direct from the *London Palladium*, from 16 September 1951 with Mr Max Wall, fresh from '*Variety Bandbox*'.

Week commencing 20 August 1951, saw the all male comedy revue '*Showboat Express*' with Britain's premier female impersonators Bartlett and Ross, and Ford (real name George William Spinks born 1907) and Sheen, (real name was Christopher Shinfield born 1908) leading the cast. (As one of their 'Misleading Ladies', Mr Danny La Rue had his first speaking part).

Week commencing 26 November, for three weeks, was Mr Prince Littler's production of '*Brigadoon*', direct from London

The list of famous names who appeared at the *Empire* is almost endless, but by the early 1950s the style of presentation was both changing and waning. Television was looming and audience tastes were rapidly changing.

From 4 September 1950, '*A Woman Desired*' was presented, adapted from the French show '*Femme Desiree*'. The *Empire* production starring Van Boolen, Denise Vane, Hazel Knight and Edwina Walton. This

Laurel and Hardy appeared at the Empire on 30 June 1952 and performed a comedy sketch entitled 'A Spot of Trouble'.

entertainment was strictly for adults only and nothing like it had ever been seen before on the English Stage!

Mr Sandy Lane, 'Yorkshire Relish' and Mr Ronnie Ronalde, (real name Ronald Charles Waldron, 1923-) singer/siffleur and famous whistler of 'In a Monastery Garden', both returned to the *Empire* in August 1951 when his act included yodelling and bird impressions.

The week commencing 17 March 1952, was the turn of Mr Al Read (1909-1987) 'Right Monkey', with assistance Miss Iris Sadler and Arthur Worsley, the ventriloquist.

From Monday 30 June 1952, the famous Hollywood film duo Laurel and Hardy, real names Arthur Jefferson (1890 - 1965) and Oliver Norvell Hardy (1882 - 1957), appeared in person at the *Empire*. They were the most recognised and loved double act of them all. Presented by Bernard Delfont they performed a comedy sketch '*A Spot of Trouble*', set in a small American town, the sketch was in two scenes. One in a railway station waiting room, the other in the Living Room of the Chief of Police. Stanley and Ollie played two travelling gents and needless to say, got into 'another fine mess'! Supporting artistes were the Lonsdale Sisters and Jimmie Elliott, animal mimic.

The week commencing 7 July saw the arrival of Mr Joseph Locke, (1918-1999) direct from his triumphant Canadian tour. Ireland's greatest tenor was over six feet tall and among other songs, gave his rendition of '*A Soldiers Dream*', and his most famous song 'I'll take you home again Kathleen'. Supporting artistes were Morecambe and Wise!

For three weeks from 3 November, Mr Edmund Hockridge appeared in the Drury Lane production of '*Carousel*', while from 22 June 1953, Miss Julie Andrews, (born 1935) real name Julia Elizabeth Wells, appeared with Mr Freddie Frinton , real name Frederick Hargate, (1911 - 1968) and Mr Max Wall in '*Cap and Belles*'. A child radio star, Miss Andrews possessed a freak four octave soprano voice. Her talent was allegedly discovered when she sang for the crowds sheltering in the London underground stations during the blitz. Be that as it may, she has the gift of lifting the spirits of an audience when she sings for them.

From Monday 24 August 1953, Noble Enterprises presented '*Celebration Rag*', with Donald Peers, Jimmy James, the Tanner Sisters and Mr Jimmy Clitheroe, real name, James Robinson Clitheroe (1916-1973). The programme cover featured a full colour photograph of Her Majesty The Queen entering the Moss Empires *London*

Miss Julie Andrews, childhood star, Sheffield Empire, June 1953.

Palladium Theatre on 3 November 1952, for a Variety Artists Benevolent Fund performance.

From 14 September, Mr David Whitfield (1926-1980) famous for 'Cara Mia', played the *Empire* and during the week commencing Monday 29 March 1954, Emile Littler presented '*Love from Judy*' starring the vivacious artiste, Miss Jean Carson. The cast also included Miss Adelaide Hall, Miss June Whitfield and Miss Barbara Windsor. Mr Arthur English (1919-1995) comedian, 'Prince of the wide boys' also appeared in variety.

Week commencing 24 April saw an appearance of the legendary Beverly Sisters, vocal trio of sisters 'Joy Teddie and Babs' all born in the early 1930s. Miss Alma Cogan (1932-1966), 'The girl with the laughing voice', appeared with Mr Michael Bentine (1922-1996) in the week commencing 26 June.

From 2 August, Pearl Carr and Teddy Johnson appeared with Mr Benny Hill, (whose real name was Alfred Hawthorn Hill 1924-1992).

Commencing 16 November, for three weeks, the *Drury Lane* production of '*South Pacific*' with Miss Patricia Hartley and Mr Nevil Whiting was presented. Miss Hartley played the part of 'Ensign Nellie Forbush' for a sixty week tour, having 480 stage shampoos in the process!

Mr Dickie Valentine (real name Richard Brice, 1930-1971) appeared at the *Empire,* week commencing 23 April 1956 and with Jimmy James and Roy Castle from 11 November 1957. He appeared at the theatre again in the week commencing 27 October 1958. He was a popular and

Singer David Whitfield with the boys club, backstage at the Lyceum.

talented artiste. His father was Dickie Maxwell, comedian.

For two weeks, from 22 October, 1956 Miss Eve Lister and Mr George Pastell appeared in the *Drury Lane* production of 'The King and I'. Across the road at the *Palace Cinema*, Union Street, the film of the same show, starring Deborah Kerr and Yul Brynner was playing during the same week! The stage show was spectacular and was enhanced by the theatre's assets of a third dimension and living intimacy. Truly this was a great musical play from Rodgers and Hammerstein with the original role of Mrs Anna immortalised by Miss Gertrude Lawrence.

From the 19 November 1956, Mr Tommy Steele (real name Thomas Hicks 1936-) appeared in the company of Mike and Bernie Winters (real brothers named Weinstein. Mike born 1927 and Bernie in 1930).

From the 6 May 1957, the *Empire*'s audiences were entertained by Mr Ken Dodd and Miss Joan Turner and from 5 August, Mr Lonnie Donegan and Mr Des O'Connor (1932-) entertained them.

The legendary Miss Shirley Bassey (1937-) appeared at the *Empire* in the week commencing 14 October, and on 15 September 1958 the *Empire* staged the musical '*Lilac Time*', starring Mr Walter Midgley.

On 2 March 1959, Jimmy Wheeler, Joe Church (1919-) front cloth comic and Chic Murray (1919-1985) appeared in variety.

Croft House Amateur Operatic Society also presented their last show at the *Empire* from 9 March 1959, this was '*The King and I*'. From 16 March, a company of emerald clad artistes presented '*Irish and Proud of It*'.

Mr John Hanson appeared in '*The Student Prince*' from the week commencing 23 March, one of the most romantic musicals by Sigmund Romberg.

After the final curtain, comedian Albert Modley sits gazing around the silent Empire auditorium for the last time, 2 May 1959.

On 30 March Mr Carroll Levis, Miss Jackie Collins and Co appeared in 'TV Star Search'.

In the week commencing 6 April, Billy Tasker appeared in 'The Lilac Domino' and the week commencing 13 April, saw the last appearance at the Empire of Jewel and Warris in 'Top of the Town'.

On 29 April, 'Me and My Girl' opened, while the week commencing 27 April 1959, saw the final presentation at the Empire Theatre.

The audience was invited to a theatre night sponsored by Smedleys tinned foods, starring Barnsley's gift to good clean fun, Mr Albert Modley.

The Empire had suffered several years of dwindling audiences and in its later years, even the most regular patrons had to admit that the neglected frontage was looking decidedly dowdy. Here was a fabulous invalid, dying but not quite dead. Even so, its closure was one more nail in the coffin of the variety theatre and its eventual demolition was much lamented by lovers of the variety theatre.

Tired, weary, sad and neglected, the Empire gave in gracefully, a grand old lady who did not even reach her three score years and ten. At sixty four years young she met a sudden and drastic demise, the impact of television finally compelling her closure. Albert Modley sat in the auditorium after the last performance gazing wistfully around the theatre after the final curtain. It was the beginning of the end that last night, Saturday 2 May, with the last first night of a great variety theatre.

A packed audience enjoyed Earl and Elgar, musical clowns and 'Big Chief Eagle Eye', drew gasps with daring feats of knife throwing and shooting. Compere, Reggie Dennis pattered through the evening with

Empire Theatre, showing Union Street side elevation, prior to demolition in 1959.

Site of the Empire in 1999, Charles Street.

competence and the JW Jackson young ladies provided a glamorous backcloth to the *Empire*'s stage. The theatre closed in preparation for demolition on Monday 4 May, having been sold for £300,000 to Murrayfield Real Estate Co, Edinburgh. The sixty four year old building was swiftly demolished the following July and replaced with a development of nineteen shops which stretched in an arc for 450 feet along Union Street, Charles Street and Pinstone Street. Estimated building costs were £125,000.

Today, these premises include, Sheffield Property shop, American Express Travel and Sugg Sportswear retailers, HMV records and several others.

Almost inevitably, the site is reputedly haunted. Rumours have it that a man was blasted from the street into one of the *Empire* turrets on the fateful night of the blitz, it is also believed that a man hanged himself in the theatre, always a good basis for a haunting! We shall never know for certain, but the ghosts of the *Empire*'s heyday will live on, immortalised in this book whose cover it so proudly graces.

THE FOLLOWING RECOLLECTIONS ARE AN EPILOGUE OF THE EMPIRE

The safety curtain which was lowered during the interval was totally covered with advertisements from local companies, the reading of which partially relieved the boredom of waiting for the second half of the show to begin. The resident manager in 1917 was Mr L.M. Stewart and in 1920-21, Iris Gibson worked in the pay box and Mr Bernard Hocking was stage door keeper for twenty years from 1938 to 1958.

When the theatre closed it was like looking at an old friend and after the last performance, the entire staff gathered on stage to a tremendous ovation from the audience. On that night the theatre was packed from stalls to circle and the 'gods'.

There was a brief speech of farewell from Mr Albert Modley.

Certainly Mrs Mildred Johnson would never forget that night. In honour of her birthday, the audience were invited to each light a match when the lights went down, creating the effect of an immense birthday cake!

Then it was all over, with a few tears and last night mourners laying

Stage door keeper Bernard Hocking holding Ukelele, with stage crew and artiste, backstage.

vocal wreaths in the otherwise silent auditorium. Mr Earnest Fenton, stage manager, found it all quite heartbreaking.

Dresser and cleaner Mrs Florrie Hirst had been there since 1925 and the Housekeeper Mrs Teresa Slim since 1927. Her first show had been 'The Golden Calf', starring Mr Raymond Massey, who later found fame in the 'Dr Kildare' television series. Mrs Doris Wood started as a cigarette girl in 1928 and after a period away, returned to the Empire in 1942 as a barmaid. She recalls that in early days, ice cream was cut from a large slab and put into wafers, later usherettes sold chock ices and Mars bars during the intervals.

Musical Director Maurice Newton joined the Empire staff in 1922. A kind caring man, the theatre was his whole life. Mrs Edna Alexander was a cloakroom attendant from 1929 and shared countless memories of the Theatre's illustrious life right up to the end when it fell in clouds of dust from bulldozers and the demolition teams.

The Empire had seen them all, from busty, gutsy Marie Lloyd whose impudent, saucy vulgarity had rung out with every charming syllable being heard at the back of the hall. Her chief rival, Miss Florrie Ford, once helped University students with their rag week events by selling bananas in Fitzalan Square. As they sang her famous song 'Yes we have no bananas', she sold 2400 of them in one hour. On another occasion she judged a competition for young boys, to see how many they could peel in a set time.

In October 1939, the students presented their rag revue 'Rags and Tatters', at the Empire, with melodrama, comedy, ballet and girls!

The theatre had seen over half a century of entertainment from grand opera to burlesque, but towards the end, shows were built around mediocre pop singers and striptease. One such presentation 'Eve', was constructed around a stripper gradually disrobing to reveal all as the seasons of the year passed by. At one stage a voice was heard to roll out from the 'gods', shouting 'Roll on December!'

Other third rate productions included 'No Orchids for Miss Blandish', a risque play and 'Follies Bergere from Paris' with Miss Vilma La Verne.

Television kept audiences at home, though in the broadest sense, theatre provided a rapport which this new media did not.

During the 1950s and at the end of its life, the Manager was Mr Johnny Spitzer. He came to the Empire straight from school, arriving wearing an old jacket frayed at the cuffs. Quite a contrast to the immaculate manager in black suit and tie. Johnny lived permanently in the Grand Hotel in Leopold Street, (built in 1910 but since demolished), and could frequently be seen in the company of the top of the bill performers, strolling round the city.

Mr Michael Brennan became a page boy at the *Empire* in 1947, at the time when Mr Lewis Pierrepont was Manager and Mr Spitzer was under manager. Michael recalls that attendants and usherettes had a nightly inspection, while outside the street would be thronged with an eager crowd and the sweet shop opposite was doing excellent business. These were the good times and the duty commisionaire would be busily directing patrons. '*Circle to your left, stalls to your right, seats in all parts!*' There he stood, resplendent in uniform, peaked cap and gold braide, in the light which cascaded so invitingly through the entrance and out onto the often wet and less than inviting pavement. Meanwhile, the billboards proudly proclaimed '*This way for the best shows in Yorkshire*'.

Miss Irene Card recalled that a former manager, Mr Joe Collins, was in fact the father of the now world famous sisters, Joan and Jackie Collins. Joe began his working life as an office boy with Moss Empires, being paid 7/6 per week. During the 1930s, a blind man called 'Knocker' Nolan sold lavender and matches outside the *Empire*, come rain hail or snow, he was always there.

Across the road in Union Street, was the *Phoenix Hotel* (in later years known as *Teddy Ross's*), where many an *Empire* star gave an impromptu performance at the bar.

On 15 December 1949, eighty permanent staff of the *Empire* were given a special bonus to mark the 50th Anniversary of Moss Empires Ltd, and as a mark of recognition of their loyalty over the years. The *Empire* ended its life with a whimper rather than a bang, as among many recollections of happier times, the fixtures and fittings went under the auctioneers hammer only one week after the closure. It is fair to say that, from the performers point of view, Sheffield was always a tough theatrical nut to crack.

On one occasion, Mr Arthur Askey (1900-1982) did no more than a short spot which included telling one or two jokes and singing the '*Silly Bee*' song before making way for the following act.

Mr Peter Harvey recalled to me how on one occasion there was an act, where the artiste Rondart (real name Ronald Romlinson born 1929) blew darts out of his mouth at targets or balloons. One night he was to be seen facing a terrified member of the audience, who had a balloon on his head. As the artiste was taking careful aim, the 'volunteer', was seen to be apparently sinking into the final stages of some terminal illness. Growing visibly paler as the moment of truth approached. It is not recorded either whether the balloon was successfully burst, or if the 'volunteer' collapsed, prior to the artiste letting fly with his dart. In those days, variety was indeed a mixed bag.

In June 1936, Mr Charlie Kunz (1896-1958) made one of several appearances at the *Empire*, playing many of his established favourites on the piano. These included '*Lily of Laguna*' and '*After the Ball*'. Later appearances at this venue by Mr Kunz were, May 1937, August 1938, 1939 and 1941, October 1944 and August 1947 and 1948. His trademark was an immaculate tail suited piano stylist. On one occasion he was supported by Miss Iris Sadler and Mr Douglas Byng (1893-1938), who would today probably be called 'The High Priest of Camp' who regaled his audiences with such ditties as 'Hot Handed Hetty' and 'Naughty Nelly Gwynn'.

In August 1939, Mr Reginald Foot played '*The Worlds Mightiest Theatre Organ*', at the *Empire*, to be followed in 1940 by Mr Harold Ramsey and his lovely ladies!

In May, 1940 the extravagant revue '*Eve on Parade*' was presented.

In October 1941, May 1944 and October 1947, the *Empire* played host to the Tom Arnold '*Hippodrome*' show, with the 'Tiller Girls' contributing to the May 1944 presentation.

Culture also played its part in the *Empire*'s programmes, with the Carl Rosa Opera Co, presenting 'Die Fledermaus', in May 1942 and 'Faust' and 'La Tosca', in their programme for June 1947. Many years before in

Letterhead of the mighty Moss Empires circuit.

April 1928, the British National Opera Co, had presented a mixed programme.

In sharp contrast, the variety programme which began in March 1932, included such great names as Will Hay, Miss Doris Hare, the Hintoni Brothers and The Five Sherry Brothers, acrobatic dancers/musicians. (Peter Sherry 1910-1979 and Sam, born 1912).

It is interesting to compare the prices charged in 1932, with those pitched to boost waning audiences in the 1948 season. 1932: Boxes £2-3-6d, Stalls 4/6d, Circle 3/8d and 4/6d, Balcony 2/. 1948: Boxes £1-7-0d, Stalls and Circle 3/6d, Balcony 9d.

During May 1928, the famous play '*Dracula*', which had enthralled London audiences, flew in to the *Empire*, while the latest revue '*Safety First*', from Mr Archie Pitt, was presented later the same month.

Among the many notable bands which performed at the *Empire* were: July 1938, Mr Jack Hylton, 'The British Master of Rhythm'; February 1937, Mr Sydney Kite, direct from the Piccadilly Hotel, London; July 1940, Jack Payne; May 1942, Oscar Rabin and Herman Darewski; June 1944, Maurice Winnick with the 'Dorchester Follies'; September 1945, Billy Cotton (1889-1969) catchphrase 'Wakey Wakey', and his Band Show and in March of the same year, Joe Loss and his Orchestra appeared. In July 1947, Geraldo and his Orchestra appeared, supported by 'Professor' Jimmy Edwards (real name James Keith O'Neil Edwards, 1920-1988)

Ever popular in Sheffield was Mr Henry Hall and his Orchestra who played the *Empire* on many occasions including; February and December 1940; March 1942; October 1944 and March 1946. This last date also included a recording of his '*Guest Night*' radio show. In this show Henry Hall was supported by Mr Clarkson Rose.

Roy Barber and his Band appeared in August 1950.

Mr Jimmy James (real name James Casey 1892-1965), appeared in May 1945, performing his famous 'drunk' sketch '*The First Night*'. On this occasion he was supported by Mr Hutton Conyers, who was billed as 'The Singing Werewolf'!

In 1942, Mr Cyril Fletcher (real name Cyril Trevellian Fletcher, 1913-) and his wife Betty Astell played the *Empire*, while in 1953, Miss Gwen Liddle, Britain's celebrated 'Street Singer', appeared with Will Carr, who juggled with his feet, in support. August 1953 also saw the appearance of the American star, Miss Rose Murphy, who had won fame with her song '*Busy Line*', with the catch line '*Brrr, Brrr, Brrr, busy line*'.

There was also a steady flow of musical productions throughout the life of the *Empire* and the following are just some of the more famous productions which were presented there:

May 1928, *The Student Prince*, which was presented again in June 1942 and November 1949. This delightful musical romance was always popular with Sheffield audiences. '*The Desert Song*' was another firm favourite which first played the *Empire* in October of 1928 and 1929, for two weeks on each occasion. The show came direct from the *Theatre Royal*, Drury Lane in 1928. The show returned in March 1930, for one week only this time.

In June 1938, Mr Harry Welchman played the title role in '*The Red Shadow*' which appeared at the *Empire*, direct from its run at the *London Coliseum*.

October 1928 and September 1929 saw the presentation of '*The Vagabond King*', while in January of 1929 '*Virginia*', starring Miss Cora Goffin, was presented.

'*Paris 1929*', was presented in May of that year, with Miss Kitty McShane in the lead, supported by Mr Arthur Lucan as '*Mrs O'Flynn*'. This act was the forerunner of Lucan's famous character 'Old Mother Riley'. Later in May the *Empire* also presented the Lawrence Tiller Girls, in '*One Damn Thing after Another*'.

September 1929 saw Julian Wylie's production of '*Mr Cinders*', with 'The Five O'Clock Girl' Miss Cora Goffin, who appeared again in '*Hold Everything*' during March 1930.

'*The Good Companions*', an adaptation of the J.B. Priestley novel was presented in February 1932 and in March 1935, '*Wild Violets*' blossomed and the Tom Arnold production of '*No No Nanette*', tapped away in March 1937.

From 19 August 1940, the great Richard Tauber made a rare personal appearance in Franz Lehar's delightful romantic operetta, '*The Land of Smiles*', in which he sang his enduring hit, '*You are My Heart's Delight*'.

In June 1946, the play with music '*The Lisbon Story*', appeared with Miss Eve Lister in the starring role and this show was followed in October by the light opera '*Merrie England*'. '*Me and My Girl*', also popped up in September 1946.

In September 1947 and again in May 1949, the Wild West came to the *Empire* with Emile Littler's production of '*Annie Get Your Gun*'.

During July 1952, Mr Barry Sinclair appeared at the *Empire* in '*King's Rhapsody*', which ran for four weeks. For many years, Sinclair was understudy to Mr Ivor Novello, who passed away in 1951 at the age of 57. (In August 1956, Tom Arnold presented this enduring Ivor Novello musical, with Mr Sinclair, Miss Olive Gilbert and Miss Zena Dare in the leading roles). Programmes for this show cost 3d and admission prices were; Boxes £2 2s 0d; Circle 6/6d; balcony 4/6d.

During September 1953, Mr Roy Barbour appeared for two weeks in

'*Zip Goes a Million*', a '*Zippy, Snappy, Happy Show*'!, direct from the *Palace Theatre*, London.

Audiences at the *Empire* saw virtually every major musical of the times, including the great masterpieces from Rodgers and Hammerstein.

Some older favourites we shall never see again, while others retain an enduring appeal and go on, seemingly forever.

In November 1953, The International Ballet Co, appeared to perform '*Copelia*' and '*Swan Lake*', direct from their triumphal tour of Spain and Italy.

In May 1955, Miss Lita Rosa, Britain's top vocalist, who had begun her career with the Ted Heath Orchestra, appeared. June that year also saw the arrival of Mr Ronnie Hilton, (real name Adrian Hill 1926-) who also appeared in March 1956 in company with Joe Black, (1918-1999) Jack Douglas (1927-) and Arthur Worsley (1920-).

'*Guys and Dolls*', came direct from a continuous run of 555 shows at the *London Coliseum*. This show was presented by Prince Littler and was based upon a story by Damon Runyan. The music was by Frank Loesser and it starred Roberta Huby and Edward Deveraux.

1955 also saw appearances in August by Miss Eve Boswell (born 1924) and in November, Mr Caroll Levis. He presented top amateur Yorkshire talent, with support from Mr Stan Stennett, (1925-) who was billed as being 'Certified, Insanely Funny'!

In December it was the turn of 'Hollywood Star Doubles', at the *Empire*. A supporting act for this show, in addition to the lookalikes was, 'Vogelbeins Real Live bears, Bruins at Their Best'. Hans Vogelbein trained and exhibited these muzzled but still dangerous bears.

The *Empire* had always offered all varieties of presentation and typically, during August 1940 the show '*Why Go To Paris?*', was presented with the effect of an intimate midnight floorshow atmosphere. The cast included the Western Brothers and Eva May Wong, plate spinner, acrobat and contortionist. This show came directly from the exclusive *Kit Kat Club* in London.

From the world of Hollywood on 30 September 1957, Mr Larry Parkes, appeared performing light comedy and singing with his wife Betty Garrett. He was famous for his portrayals of Al Jolson in '*The Jolson Story*' and '*Jolson Sings Again*'. Miss Sadie Macnamarra clarinet player extraordinare recalled playing the *Empire* with singer Mr Victor Gilling.

Pantomime was an important part of the annual bill of fare offered by the *Empire*. From the opening date of 1895

Miss Sadie Macnamarra and Mr Victor Gilling.

until 1912, the pantomime as an entertainment, did not exist. The first 'panto', offered by the *Empire* was, almost inevitably, '*Cinderella*', which was presented for the Christmas season in December 1913. This was followed by a break of three years with no pantomime, but December 1917, saw '*Little Bo Peep*' being staged. There was a further gap until 1920, when '*Cinderella*' was presented again. Following '*Jack and Jill*' in 1921, the *Empire* presented an annual pantomime, with the exceptions of 1933 and 1942, the latter being as a result of bomb damage. In addition to the Christmas 'panto's', there were a number of out of season shows including: '*Snow White and the Seven Dwarfs*' which ran from 6 February 1939 and '*Robinson Crusoe*', which on this occasion was presented by Bertram Montague, from 15 January 1940. This show included 'Eugene's Flying Ballet'. From Tuesday 3 March 1942, Miss Barbara Mullen, later to portray 'Janet' in the long running '*Dr Finlays Casebook*', starred in the title role in '*Peter Pan*', while Alistair Sim was 'Captain Hook' and Joan Greenwood played 'Wendy'. 'Mrs Darling' was played by Miss Zena Dare.

'*Little Red Riding Hood*', was presented from 9 January 1933 and back in 1913, Sir Joseph Beecham presented a visit to '*The Golden Land of Fairy Tales*', daily at 2.00pm. This included highlights from '*Puss in Boots*'; '*Red Riding Hood*'; '*The Sleeping Beauty*' and '*Snowdrop*'.

From 30 December 1912, John Tiller Presented '*Cinderella*', for one week only. Other pantomimes to grace the stage of the *Empire* included: 1932. '*Aladdin*', with Dan Leno Junior as 'Widow Twankey' and Jenny Hartley in the title role. This magnificent production was presented by Frances Laidler, with a brilliant cast and a splendid West End chorus.

In 1936, '*Cinderella*', appeared again with Jay Laurier as 'Buttons' and Marion Wilson in the title role. Patricia Burke was 'Dandini' and the show had a supporting company of over 100 artistes.

In 1938, Tessie O'Shea (1914-1995) was in '*Dick Whittington*' and 1939 saw the arrival of '*Ali Baba and the Forty Thieves*', with Vincent Lawson as 'Ali' and Rita Bernard as his son 'Ganem'. The show was sprinkled with topical wartime allusions to food rationing and depth charges. It was presented three times daily for two weeks.

In 1944, Mr Shaun Glenville and Miss Dorothy Ward starred in '*Jack and the Beanstalk*' and in 1945, Bertram Montague presented his third spectacular pantomime '*The Babes in the Wood*', with Jimmy Jewel and Ben Warris as 'The Robbers'. The Montague presentation for 1946 was '*Mother Goose*', with Hy Hazel as 'Colin' and Albert Modley in the title role. Following his emergence from the magic pool of youth, beautifully transformed, he proceeded to play a drum kit, which just happened to be close by. To coin one of Modleys own catchphrases, '*Flippin Ek!*'

The pantomime 'Humpty Dumpty' performed in 1951, featured the Tiller Girls, snowflake ballet.

In 1948, the great showman, Mr Emile Littler, took over the pantomime reins at the *Empire* in order to present the all laughter pantomime '*Aladdin*'. Nat Mills was 'Widow Twankey' and Bobbie Mills played 'Wishee Washee'. The unknown newcomer in the show Miss Jean Carson, who later took London by storm in '*Love from Judy*', played 'Aladdin'. The John Tiller Girls also made one of their many appearances in 'panto' at the *Empire*.

In 1949, '*Little Bo Peep*', lost her sheep again in the company of Dave and Joe O'Gorman, as 'Simple Simon' and 'Dame Trott', the Tiller Girls were once more in attendance.

In 1951 it was '*Humpty Dumpty*', falling off the wall as Albert Modley looked on as 'King Yolk of Eggville' and the Tillers once more 'strutted their stuff'.

Tommy Fields (real name Thomas 1908-1988) topped the bill as '*Mother Goose*' in 1952, a very tall man, he was really more suited to variety than the part of a pantomime dame. The Chevalier Brothers, a two-handed comedy acrobatic act, played the 'Village Policemen', with Curries 'Fairy Waterfall' and of course, the Tillers.

In 1953, '*Cinderella*', once more climbed into her golden coach, accompanied by Desmond and Marks as the 'Ugly Sisters'. Again the Tillers were in evidence, while Albert Modley stood by as 'Buttons'.

1954 saw '*Goody Two Shoes*', with Sonny Jenks as 'Bluebell', the old woman who lived in a shoe. Medlock and Marlow as 'Twiggie and Muddles', the Tillers of course and 'A Wild Woofum Puff', played by himself. Let's face it, anything goes in pantomime!

In 1955, '*Jack and Jill*', somehow managed to get involved with a crooked sixpence, while Charlie Chester (1914-1997) played himself and Kathleen West was 'Dame Trot'. Sid Plummer was 'Twist' and the now famous Tiller Girls showed numerous legs!

In 1956, it was that all laughter show '*Aladdin*' again. In this production, Nat Jackley played 'Widow Twankey', while Jimmy Clitheroe was 'Wishee Washee'. As ever, those Tiller Girls were there. There is a story, which may or may not be true, but it runs as follows. Mr Issy Bonn, (real name Benny Levin 1903-1977) the Jewish singer with a powerful voice who peppered his act with jokes about the Finklefetter family, was given a guest spot in '*Aladdin*'. He played an unnamed character who appeared when Aladdin rubs his lamp. Aladdin's first wish is alleged to have been for Issy to sing '*My Yiddisher Momma*'!

In 1957, '*Little Miss Muffet*', was frightened by a spider, while in the company of world famous clown, Charlie Carioli (1910-1980) and in December 1958, the *Empire* presented its very last 'panto', '*Babes in the Wood*', starring Laurie London and Edna Savage as the 'Babes', Billy Burdon as 'Simple Simon' and Sheffield's own Roy Barbour in the dame role, which for this show was 'Nurse'. Helen James as 'Robin Hood', made her entrance in a flowing green cloak. According to Mr Richard L. Roper, who saw this production when aged seven, she came on stage

Tiller Girls perform a ballet scene in the pantomime 'Goody Two Shoes', 1954.

to the tune of '*Robin Hood, Robin Hood, Riding through the glen.....*', from the long running series of *Robin Hood* then appearing on television. He also recalls the blue nursery steps 'collapsing', as the robbers ran up them in their attempts to kidnap the 'Babes', while 'Eugenes Flying Ballet', flew right out from the stage to the Circle during their 'Journey to Butterfly Land'! which drew gasps from the audience.

When the final curtain fell, the wicked robber smiled shyly and said, '*Goodbye Edna*'. It was one of the many goodbyes at the *Empire* when the curtain fell for the 71st time after the 'babes' had diced with death yet again, and won.

'Stinker', the rabbit was back in his hutch and it was goodbyes all round between fellow troupers, though nobody cried or opened a consolation bottle to say goodbye to an old friend whose days were numbered. Stage, it was not long before '*Sherwood Forest*', was deftly dismantled and the jubilant voices of green clad outlaws were replaced with silence. A silence which would only be broken in future by the sound of pneumatic drills, hissing acetylene cutters and steam hammers, all harmonised in a cruel concerto in their act of destroying Sheffield's home of variety.

Roy Barbour appeared at the *Empire* for the first time in 1911, at the age of seven and made his farewell appearance on the same stage. He said, '*Closing the theatre is a tragedy, I shall miss it very much*'. The final pantomime had as ever been presented by Emile Littler, who had presented the Tiller Girls in almost every one of his shows at the *Empire* since 1948. After '*Goody Two Shoes*' in 1954/55, at the suggestion of Shirley Harris, (nee Hussey), several of the girls decided to meet up in Sheffield every five years. Their first reunion in 1960, was on the site of the *Empire*, but subsequent gatherings have taken place at the *Grosvenor House Hotel*.

The remaining members of the group are: Olive Peutrell, (nee Lowe); Jean Smith; Pam Harcourt, (nee Hoult); Elizabeth Barrett; Beryl Smith and Pat Marriott. Sheffield born Pam Hoult was head girl of the 1955 troupe. She recalls that they were a friendly group of 16 and the dancing was very hard work, but they all enjoyed the guardsman like precision of it all.

In 1952, the casts of the *Empire* and *Lyceum* were invited to the Town Hall, were they received a tour of the Civic Plate by the Lord Mayor. The performers present included: Albert Modley, Roberta Huby, Pam Holt from the *Empire* and Harry Secombe from the *Lyceum*. Shirley Hussey was very fond of Sheffield and said that the pantomimes were always a popular attraction. She did five consecutive years at her beloved *Empire* and Pam Harcourt did three. Her first professional show was '*Humpty*

Dumpty', in the 1951 season, during which, at the age of 16, she earned £6 10s 0d per week. Pam ended her career at the *London Palladium*, working with Harry Secombe in the revue '*Large as Life*'. In between her appearances in '*Large as Life*', she also high kicked her way through three Royal Variety Shows!

Pam also organised a grand reunion to mark the 1/4 century since their retirement from the stage. This was for Tiller Girls everywhere and on 24 October 1981, over 250 of them turned up. The long legged lovelies of the 1950s, famed for their high kick routines, enjoyed this memorable occasion. Following an afternoon buffet, several of them were encouraged to re-live the high kick when the resident disc jockey played the *Can Can*. Fond memories of the past were recalled and everyone who attended got a kick out of the whole affair.

The seven girls from the *Empire* troupe, still meet every five years in Sheffield to keep the memory of the *Empire* alive and to keep up on the current affairs in each other's lives. Their next meeting is in December 1999, when it is hoped they will be in attendance for the signing of this book at the Starstore in Sheffield.

It is interesting in closing, to recall a brief history of the Tiller Girls, who began in 1890, the inspiration of John Tiller.

At Easter 1900, the 'Tiller Quartet', known as 'The Four Sunbeams' appeared at the *Winter Gardens Theatre* in Blackpool. Their numbers grew with their fame and when he died in October 1925, troupes bearing his name were still high kicking their way through what was to become

The Tiller Girls re-union, from left to right: Jean Smith, Shirley Harris, Beryl Smith, Elizabeth Barret, Olive Peutrell, Pat Marriott and Pam Harcourt.

a century of dancing tradition and into the hearts of audiences everywhere, who revered their skill and precision. (In that 1900 show 'Jack Ashore', a patriotic spectacle, the Tillers began a long association with Blackpool, with queues around the block every night to see them. They worked under the ever watchful eye of Jennie Walker, John Tiller's second wife. In those early days, there were no tights suitable for their routines, so they put 'wet white', a gooey mixture of glycerine and oxide, on their legs when on stage).

They were part of the first ever commercial television broadcast from London and are best remembered from their regular television spot in 'Sunday Night at the London Palladium'. Undoubtedly, this revitalised their fame and as a result they thrived during the 1960s. They also appeared in 'The Crazy Gang Show', 'Young at Heart' and during the run of 'The Five Past Eight Show', in Glasgow, were obliged to travel to London every Sunday for their spot in the 'Palladium', show.

The presence of the Tillers in any show always heralded an excellent performance all round and packed houses as a result. In 1978, they once again returned to Blackpool to appear at the Opera House Theatre, this time wearing tights. John Tiller's son Lawrence, opened up in competition with his father during the 1920s, assisted by his wife Amy, but he retired from the business in 1936. John Tiller's girls were considered to be more sophisticated than Lawrence's and even today, there is friendly rivalry between the two groups when they meet. The strangest setting in which the Tiller Girls ever performed, was on a raft in the harbour at Monte Carlo. Rather like Miss Jean Brodie's girls, the Tillers were always considered to be 'The Creme de la Creme'.

Empire and Lyceum pantomime casts, with the Lord Mayor of Sheffield. Sir Harry Secombe, CBE, second row right; Albert Morley to his left. Pam Harcourt and Roberta Huby two to his right. January 1952.

THE THEATRE ROYAL

Located at the corner of Tudor Street and Arundel Street. On 16 June 1761, plans were made to raise by subscription £3,600, in order to build a new playhouse and Assembly Rooms. They were built back to back in 1762, the theatre frontage was in Norfolk Street and the back in Tudor Place.

The playhouse opened in 1763 and being worthy of the name new 'theatre' was the pride of the town. Seating 800, this large and commodious theatre was handsomely decorated and had excellent scenery. The Assembly Rooms contained a dance hall and gaming room, featuring three cut-glass lustres of elegant design. Managed by Michael

The Theatre Royal, Tudor Street with Adelphi Hotel opposite.

Heaton and Joseph Austen of Newcastle, the theatre opened with a performance of 'The Provoked Wife' by William Congreave.

In 1769, the theatre was utilised in conjunction with St Paul's Parish Church, demolished in 1938, to hold a 'Grand Musical Festival'. Handel's 'Messiah' and 'Acis and Galatea', were performed. Ninety eight instrumentalists and one hundred and sixty vocalists took part. Other festivals of a similar type were also presented from time to time.

In 1773, rebuilding proposals were made and on 6 May 1776, it was announced that a new theatre was to be built in Tudor Street. The old theatre was demolished and a foundation stone for the new building was laid on 6 August 1777.

The Theatre Royal seating plan.

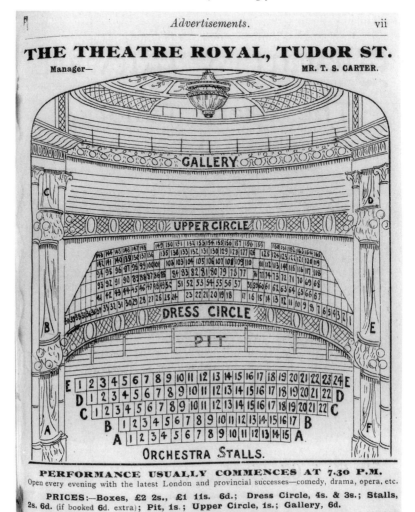

Opening in 1778, its successor was renamed the *'Theatre Royal'* and was a much more spacious edifice fitted out in an elegant manner. It was, however, criticised for its architect's bad design and poor acoustics. The Assembly Rooms were absorbed in its construction. Despite the dramatic internal and external changes, there remained on the front of the building, the spirited profile of Shakespeare and other dramatic symbols which had been executed for the original builders by a poor wandering man called Renilowe.

The theatre was managed by actor and owner, Mr William Herbert and was originally intended for legitimate plays, but several musical performances and ballad operas were also staged there. A small orchestra was recruited from local musicians and led for many years by Mr Joseph Taylor, who came from a well-known musical family.

On 4 April 1781, the presentation was again Handel's *'Acis and Galatea'*, with a violin concerto performed by a Mr Lawton, an organist from Rotherham. This was presented at reduced prices: Boxes 2/-, Pit 1/6 and Gallery 1/-. Books and wax lights could be bought at the theatre.

This was a period of great depression in Sheffield and though well patronised in early days, the theatre had a perpetual struggle to maintain its audiences, despite the fact that the proprietor appears to have 'reaped a fair harvest'. For three seasons the new theatre was not managed well by Mr Herbert. It was then taken over by Mr James Shafto Robinson who did even worse. By way of improvement, the year 1781 was a landmark for Sheffield's theatrical history when the town came within the York circuit under the renowned, Tate Wilkinson. Several members of the Blonk family were theatrical proprietors and Wilkinson approached Benjamin Blonk, merchant and theatre steward, with a view to renting the theatre for an entire season, three years after taking control. Blonk assured him that he would command large audiences but wanted such a large slice of the cake in profits that Wilkinson did not go ahead. Receipts had not been impressive and instead the theatre was taken over by William Pero who remained there for five years.

He presented on 9 October 1787, *'The Revenge and Harlequin's Triumph'* featuring the scenes and machinery taken from the *Theatre Royal,* Covent Garden, London. He presented the show for thirty nights! An unusual feature within a varied programme over the seasons, was the addition of the dancing of a hornpipe at the end of *'Macbeth'* Act IV!

A realistic representation of an air balloon flight was depicted in 'The Sorrows of Werther', which was followed by *'Much Ado About Nothing'*.

Music had a place too in the theatre's repertoire, with a visit of an Italian Company from *Sadler's Wells.*

'*Alfred*', a historical tragedy by Ebenezer Rhodes, was unsuccessful and in 1789, the theatre was taken over by the Chester based partnership of Charles Whitlock and Joseph Shepherd Munden.

Many famous actors trod the boards here, one of the first being the famous and beautiful Miss Sarah Siddons, from London. She broke through the prejudice of the time, which regarded starring in provincial theatre as degrading. In 1789, she achieved great success in '*Jane Shore*' and was to return to the *Theatre Royal* again in 1799. Immortalised by Sir Joshua Reynolds, her towering genius was marked by a wall plaque on the former *Theatre Royal*, Bath. Her brothers, Stephen and Charles Kemble, were also associated with the theatre. Because of his enormous size, Stephen played 'Falstaff' in 1790, without the need for padding! He took over the company in January 1791. The younger brother, Charles, made his debut, in 1792 as 'Orlando', continuing his association with Sheffield until 1827. He married a Miss de Camp, who was noted for acting and dancing in pantomime.

She had previously been a prime favourite in Royal circles. The shows '*No Supper, No Song*', '*The Dramatist*' and '*Gallic Freedom*', a play of spectacular proportions about the French revolution, were not successful.

However, Kemble and the company (which still included Whitlock), received great compliment. The regular season in 1791 opened with '*The Beggars Opera*', and '*The Irish Widow*', but neither produced good box office. The house filled so ill each night that there were considerable losses. At this point, Kemble introduced 'the effect of novelty in pieces', with '*The Surrender of Calais*' and '*Wild Oats*'. A local man, Mr Creswick, a great admirer of himself, played the title role in 'Richard III'.

In 1792, having produced little that was outstanding and due to heavy expenses, Kemble took his final bow and left Sheffield. Under Mr Pero's management, was shortly presented the comedy '*Everyone has his Fault*'. At this time the theatre underwent a judicious alteration producing a beautiful appearance in the house, with the renovated box fronts, scenes and wings.

From 1794, a Mr Taylor controlled presentations until his death in 1798. Disturbances in the theatre were instigated by John 'Jacky' Blackwell, a tailor who had headed the bread rioters in the troubled times of 1816-1821. His interruptions earned him the title 'King of the Gallery'!

Shafto Robertson appeared in '*The Few*' and in September 1798, '*The Sultan*', which raised £50 for the Royal Infirmary. Orchestra leader, Taylor, who had assisted Robertson, died and from 1799, the point of Siddon's welcome return, the *Theatre Royal* prospered under Mr J.W.

Macready, a famous name in theatrical circles.

The grand spectacle 'Timour the Tartar', produced a novelty in 1815. The story of 'The Forest of Bardy' (alternatively 'Dog of Montargis'), revolved around an assassin pursued by a dog 'Tiger' who eventually shoots him with a pistol! Superb theatre, which no doubt held the attentive audiences spellbound!

Audiences of the period expected long, spectacular programmes featuring strong melodramas, which they certainly got and such plays formed a great part of the *Theatre Royal*'s programming. This plus a wealth of talent established its reputation. Around the early 1800s, it gained the reputation of being one of the foremost provincial playhouses.

In 1805, a play was performed partly in the St Paul's Parish Church and partly in the Theatre. The proceeds raised in aid of the infirmary, totalled £833, which after expenses, made them £306. Admission prices in the theatre were: Boxes 7/-, Pit 3/6 and Gallery 2/6. In view of the level of wages earned by the ordinary Sheffielder, in those days, it is unlikely that many of them saw this presentation.

In 1811, a benefit presentation featured a Mr Wilson performing a high wire act by pushing a wheelbarrow on a tightrope from the stage up to the gallery and down again!

On Wednesday 8th December 1809, there was another presentation of the play 'Jane Shore', with Mrs Patrick Campbell in the title role. 'Once a Tour De Force, Now Forced to Tour', was her famous quote. On the same bill was Mr Martin, comic singer with a rendition of 'John Lump's trip to Sheffield Fair', and a farce 'Two Strings to your Bow' (or the pudding is in the eating).

Other famous players of the time included Edmund Kean, John Litton and Munden, a great comedian who was at his height at the time of the Battle of Waterloo in 1812. On 8 December 1825, a German play and melodrama 'The Keeper's Daughter' was staged requiring a tank of water and a ten foot long boat on stage to simulate a storm at sea.

Charles Dickens visited the *Surrey Street Music Hall* in 1852 with a celebrity company to raise funds for the 'Guild of Literature and Arts'. With the stage presentation having the *Theatre Royal* staff assisting, it was a great success.

It was the custom to give triple or double bills at Christmas, hence, on Christmas Eve 1827, a double bill was presented, comprising the plays 'The Tragedy of Wallace' and 'The Idiot Witness'. Not very cheerful Christmas entertainment and on Boxing Day the mood was maintained with 'Richard III', followed by 'Golvas' on 27 December.

In 1855, the interior was entirely rebuilt at a cost of £30,000. The outer walls were retained, while the reconstruction of the general edifice was executed by Architects Messrs Flockton and Sons, Sheffield. The stage was constructed by Mr Straughan, of London.

During 1856, the Italian Opera Company, The English Opera Company and The London Grand Opera, all appeared at the *Theatre Royal* with such popularity that a playbill of the time stated '*Arrangements will be made with the Railway Companies for special trains from neighbouring towns!*'.

On 28 November 1878, Sir Henry Irving appeared at the *Theatre Royal* to great acclaim. There was a packed house, so full that people were turned away. The programme opened with '*The Bells*', a dramatisation of Monsieur M. Erokmaan-Chatrian's terrible novel. Irving played a man who murders a Polish Jew, his character being the Burgomaster Mathias. Needless to say he executed the part with great artistic merit. In '*Jingle*', adapted from Dicken's '*Pickwick Papers*', he portrayed Alfred Jingle and kept the entire house roaring with laughter the whole time. Irving also performed '*Hamlet*' excerpts with Maude Brennan as '*Ophelia*' and '*Louis XI*'.

The Carl Rosa Opera Company also played the *Theatre Royal* in 1878, presenting '*The Merry Wives of Windsor*' and '*The Lily of Killarney*', a rare gem. Madame's Comic Opera Company opened that year with Offenbach's '*Genevieve de Brabant*' and '*Carmen*'. Mr Sullivan gave several songs, notably '*Wearing of the Green*' and '*St Patrick*', to the evident delight of the house.

Charles Dillon, a fine actor appeared in May 1879 as '*Othello*', (when he appeared here in 1881 as '*Macbeth*', Dillon would throw a cloak over his costume with a theatrical gesture and , 'popped across the road', to the *Adelphi* public house!) A Mr Chippendale (no relation to the furniture maker) also appeared with his wife who was a comedienne.

A noteworthy production was Charles Reade in a version of '*Put Yourself in his Place*', about the trades outrages.

Occasionally, acrobatic acts would be featured: 'Yokohama' a Japanese high-wire artiste, climbed from stage right up to gallery using only his toes! (There was no safety net to prevent accident to artiste or audience!).

Humour sometimes invaded the realms of serious drama, years before the famous pantomimes were established.

During the management of Mr Charles Webb, Mr L (anonymity preserved) prevailed upon him to let him play 'Polonius'. Mr L was a High Street fish dealer and came the night of his presentation, all went well until the line '*Dost know me Lord?*' With a sly wink to the audience, Webb replied '*Excellent well , you are a fishmonger*'. The ensuing laughter reached a crescendo when Mrs L, jumped up from her box seat and exclaimed '*If my 'usband is, you've no need to throw it in his face!*' The end result can only be imagined.

Inevitably, the varied programme included '*Sherlock Holmes*' plays and Edgar Wallace's '*The Wrecker*' and '*The Terror*'.

The *Theatre Royal* had it all, pigeons, performing dogs and even Arab horses in '*The Still Alarm*'. In a masterly touch of melodrama, a lady was thrown into a simulation of 'fiery furnace', in '*Ace of Trumps*', while in '*Little Vagabonds*' a cruel gypsy threw 'boulders', to scar the leading lady! Indeed those were the days! The list of artistes appearing is seemingly endless and many of them became part of the *Theatre Royal*'s history as well as stars.

To mention a few: the greatest clown Joseph Grimaldi (1778 - 1837), 'The King of Clowns', 'Dan Leno', 'George Arliss', 'The Marlboroughs', 'Claude Rains' and not forgetting Bransby Williams, 'Mona Vivian' and a great lady of the theatre Elaline Terriss', who appeared in '*Quality Street*', by J.M. Barrie. Henry Lytton, the great Shakespearian actor, Sir Frank Benson and the celebrated Savoyard Darrel Fancourt also appeared.

On 29 November 1897, a film of Queen Victoria's Diamond Jubilee procession was shown, supported by the stage production '*Morocco Bound*'.

A 'Vitograph' interlude was slotted into the pantomime '*Babes in the Wood*', on 7 January 1898. (Apart from the earlier 'animated pictures', the only other occasion that film was presented, occurred on 1 July 1924, when a travelogue '*Through Romantic Italy*', was shown. A lecturer accompanied the film in the theatre).

Mr Bransby Williams (1870-1961) famous for Dickensian characterisations.

Mr F.W. Purcell acquired the theatre in 1897. In 1901, the *Theatre Royal* was closed for five weeks. A complete renovation took place inside and out, Mr Purcell having this fine theatre completely redecorated. The architect, Mr Frank Matcham, wisely retained the existing colour scheme, which defied improvement. The entrance hall mouldings, panel paintings and staircase were unchanged structurally but entirely repainted. Likewise the auditorium ceiling and balcony mouldings and indeed all parts of the house were enhanced. Combined with a new electrical system more in keeping with modern requirements, the overall result was aesthetically brighter and of a cheering effect. A new heating system using hot water pipes was installed, draughts at doorways were greatly reduced and every part of the theatre was now warm and comfortable. For the same reason, draught reduction, curtains were introduced between the grand circle and refreshment bar and in other places where they had previously not existed. Upholstered seats were introduced in the Pit and upper Circle so that patrons would no longer sweat and groan on a weary wooden bench. Few theatres in the country would now be as comfortable as the *Theatre Royal*'s second class areas.

The most radical structural alterations were to the stage, which was increased in depth by 25ft. Greatly enlarged, it now measured 66ft wide and 45ft deep. Neither was the comfort of the actors overlooked and the old dressing rooms were demolished, to be replaced with comfortable new ones.

Development of the theatre's resources helped to make it a really first class venue. Having excellent stage connections, Mr Purcell embarked upon an enterprising policy of presentations. Mr Forbes-Robertson and London Company (plays), presented Mrs Lili Langtry in 'The Royal Necklace', Miss Julia Nielson in 'Sweet Nell of Old Drury' and Mrs Lewis Waller in 'Zasa'. Mr Mouillott's Company made a return visit with 'The Geisha', 'The Runaway Girl' and 'A message from Mars'. They also staged the latest American musical extravaganza 'The Girl from up There'.

In 1903, strenuous efforts were made to raise funds for the establishment of a University in Sheffield. To support this endeavour, Mr Charles Manners 'Moody-Manners', company presented a week of operatic productions.

From 14 November 1904, 'Faust', 'Carmen', and three Wagner Opera's were staged with a company of eminent soloists accompanied by an eighty five strong chorus and sixty piece orchestra. The resulting £457 raised, was added to the appeal fund. During the 1914-18 War, the *Theatre Royal* continued to stage operas and melodrama which even in these difficult times, were very well attended. The pay box sign quite often read 'Standing Room Only'.

In 1918, the *Theatre Royal*, along with the *Lyceum Theatre* opposite, were both by Managing Director John E.B. Beaumont and managed by Mr John Hart.

Smoking in the auditorium was authorised by the stage committee and the management made every provision for the comfort of patrons by extracting the smoke with electric fans. For patrons convenience, ashtrays were fixed in all parts of the house. Always described as a commodious structure, the *Theatre Royal*'s internal arrangement presented a happy combination of comfort and elegance. The theatre was lit throughout by electricity. During the years of grace that followed, the theatre maintained its reputation for excellence, with a wide variety of first class dramatic plays and pantomimes.

In 1876, the pantomime was '*The Man in the Moon*'.

One of the best pantomimes presented, in 1878, was '*Aladdin*'. The cast was Miss Madge Antoinette in the title role and Mr E.M. Robson as 'The Widow'. Mr E.W. Marshall played 'Pill Garlic'.

In 1884, '*Sinbad the Sailor*', featured a balloon ride over Sheffield on stage and in 1886 '*Robinson Crusoe*' was performed.

The *Theatre Royal* was Sheffield's most renowned home of pantomime, which was presented every year from '*Dick Whittington*', in 1891 to '*Red Riding Hood*', in 1927, with the exception of 1898 when pantomime was omitted from the Christmas programme. Always a popular choice with audiences, '*Cinderella*', the favourite tale of a luckless kitchen wench turned princess, was presented four times in 1893, 1903, 1912 and 1919.

There were unusual pantomimes too, '*The Forty Thieves*', in 1896, '*Bo Peep*', in 1901, with '*Sinbad the Sailor*' again in 1911. '*The House that Jack Built*' in 1913 and '*Tom, Tom the Piper's Son*', in 1922.

The 1909 '*Jack and Jill*' and 1910 '*Jack and the Beanstalk*', were both written with great success by J. Hickory Wood, '*Jack and the Beanstalk*' in particular had a phenomenally large cast. These gorgeous pantomimes were presented by John Hart, whose skills were augmented by 'beautiful scenery and electrical effects'.

Mr Rowland Hill was secured, in the face of competing offers from the principal pantomimes of Manchester, Leeds and Bradford, to play the widowed dame 'Mother Muggles'. Miss Nell Emerald who had a wealth of ability from her time in musical comedy was the principal boy 'Jack'. The cow was manipulated by two continental acrobats, the 'Valdo Brothers'. The village sweep was played by one of the best coon delineators of the day, 'Mr Kit Keen'. The King of Coonland was played by the Lilliputian actor 'Master McCraig'. Latest songs included '*On the silvery sands*' and '*I feel so lonely*'. Admission prices, at this time were: Dress Circle 3/-, Stalls 2/6. The telephone number for advance bookings was 193!

For many years, the *Theatre Royal* attracted pantomime lovers from all over South Yorkshire and it is easy to see why, from the above presentation which was typical of the very highest standard of theatrical entertainment.

The 1913 pantomime featured 'Jack-all tattered and torn' and 'Aunt

Purdy', the 'old woman who lived in a shoe' and a 'House' built of giant playing cards that collapsed on stage! Fairies, policemen, milkmaids, Lords and Ladies and nymphs, all contributed to another successful *Theatre Royal* season. Returning briefly to the 1909 pantomime, 'Jack', the eldest son was played by Miss Ella Retford and 'Jill', the runaway Princess by Miss Josie Delaine. 'Dame Horner' , a widow through no fault of her own, by Jack Cromo. 'Snap and Shott', the handymen, were played by 'The Haytors' and 'the Colleen' by Miss Irene Le Fre. A racehorse, 'The Loser' was played by a real horse, himself! Fabulous scenic effects included 'The Hill and Fairy Well', 'The Sunflower Glade' and 'The Hall of the Knights'.

These insights into the pantomimes of the day, serve to compare with those of the 1990s but there is little comparison when one marvels at the *Theatre Royal*'s stupendous presentations! The programme gives us a valuable insight, also, into prices and audience comforts of the time. For example, *Cadbury*'s chocolate was on sale in the theatre, the celebrated exhibition packets being 1/- and 2/- each. The Irish Linen Company, sold shirt collars for 2/3d per half dozen. Hay and Son, Norfolk Street, sold Scotch Whiskies at 4/- per bottle! 'Fisher's' meat pies could be obtained at the theatre bars for 2d each! A souvenir brochure of the pantomime with photographs of principal artistes was also sold for 2d.

Compare these to the admission prices which were popular: Private boxes £2 2s 0d, Grand Circle 2/6, Stalls 2/-, Pit Stalls 1/- , Pit and Upper Circle 6d and Gallery 4d! Early opening at 6.30pm and entrance to the Gallery was by the 'ordinary', door in Arundel Street.

A particularly memorable pantomime of this time, probably the 1927 '*Little Red Riding Hood*', featured 'Kirbys Flying 'Ballet', with 'Butterflies', (on wires as in '*Peter Pan*'), flying over the stalls (founded by George Kirby in 1904 and continued by his son Joe). In addition there was a Highland Scene with tartan clad dancers and waterfalls.

There were no pantomimes from 1928 to 1935, though Sangers Circus of six lions appeared frequently just before Christmas on variety bills.

After the show, the place for a drink was the *Adelphi Hotel* just opposite the *Theatre* at 13 Arundel Street. A Stones beer house, it was very popular with the stage people from the *Theatre Royal* and *Lyceum*. Its frontage bearing the name '*Adelphi*', came from the 1858 *Adelphi Theatre* in the Strand, London. Their motto was '*If its worth selling, we sell it*'. Licensee was Mr W. Banning. This externally imposing establishment had double entrance doors at the corner of Sycamore Street (long since demolished, '*The Crucible Theatre*', now stands on its site).

Pianos used at the *Theatre Royal* at this time were supplied by John

Hoyland, Piano and Organ dealers, established in 1859. They were located opposite the *Albert Hall* in Barker's Pool. (The premises were demolished to make way for the new City Hall, along with several other buildings. The City Hall opened on 22 September 1932).

The 1909 scenery canvas, gauze and draperies were rendered chemically fire-resistant with 'Boram' and for the convenience of patrons, the programme contained a tram timetable of last cars to each city terminus. Even football matches were detailed! On 19 February 1909, the United Reserves played Mexborough!

In conclusion, it is quite apparent that every effort was made by the *Theatre Royal* management to ensure a complete night's entertainment for its valued patrons. Such was the tradition for stage presentations and service of the highest calibre which had always been maintained, in the fascinating history of the *Theatre Royal*. In 1927, Ivor Novello appeared in his play '*The Rat*', which enthralled audiences. In January, 1930, Sheffield's arch villain, Charles Peace was made even more notorious when a play, based on his life, was produced. Members of the legal profession who had defended him at the York trial, in 1879, were present in the audience.

On Monday 10 March 1930, Mr Barry O'Brien's company presented '*77 Park Lane*'. On Monday 17 March, the musical play '*The Birds Nest*' was staged. Towards the end of its life, the *Theatre Royal* changed

The Theatre Royal ablaze on the night of 30 December, 1935.

The Lyceum Theatre (left) and the ruin of the Theatre Royal.

to variety presentations.

The world's smallest working car was photographed outside the *Theatre Royal* in June 1935 as a publicity stunt. At the end of the week, Mr Chris Charlton, illusionist, attempted to make the car disappear. The result of his effort is not recorded!

The history of the *Theatre Royal* was somewhat romantic, it was the oldest Sheffield theatre specifically built for the purpose. From the sizzling limelights, illuminating a world of fantasy, to the twentieth century, the *Theatre Royal* maintained a position of prominence in

Sheffield's theatre history.

However, it was sizzling flames which were to bring about the downfall of the second oldest theatre, in England. The performance of '*Castellis Accordian Band*', on Friday 29 December 1935, was over and the audience had long since gone home when tragedy struck, in the early hours of Sunday 31 December! A fire broke out in the theatre and soon the top of the building was like a colossal blast furnace. Flames were licking everywhere with embers flying in all directions and quantities of slates hurtling down into the roadway. Under the direction of Mr Breaks, Fire Brigade Chief, the firemen did a splendid job, but to no avail. Neither the fire chief or Mr Arthur Holland, theatre manager, could believe their eyes at the speed with which the fire's intensity increased. Even though some thirty firemen had arrived quickly on the scene and valiantly played numerous hoses onto the blaze, they could do little to save the theatre. Within an hour, virtually nothing remained of the interior. The three balconies and entire seating, were all reduced to debris. The interior was gutted though the stage remained almost untouched, but falling debris damaged the scenery and musical instruments left in place over the weekend. At the height of the fire, people living in houses nearby were evacuated in case the fire spread to their homes, so intense was the heat. Precautions were also taken to stop it spreading to the adjoining *Lyceum Theatre* and *Adelphi Pub* buildings, by playing water onto them. The vision of the *Theatre Royal* wafted

The shell of the Theatre Royal, the morning after the fire of 31 December.

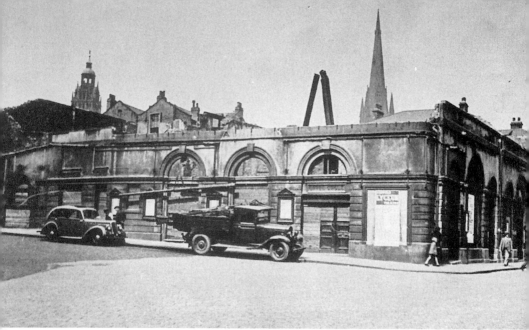

The Theatre Royal, after partial demolition.

away in flames, its 'death' was a heartbreaking sight for the large crowd of onlookers. It had been loyally supported by a regular audience over the years, since Messrs Austin and Heaton first commenced operations. The 'Gods', had given many of the older generation their first introduction to the world of the theatre. Thus, within days of its 157th birthday, Sheffield's oldest landmark perished.

The fire left the outer walls in a dangerous condition causing traffic to be diverted away from Tudor Street and Arundel Street. All dangerous walls etc, were quickly demolished leaving only the old perimeter walls and the prop room. (Ironically, the original Shakespeare profile on the front had remained undamaged and was rescued intact from the ruins. Had the *Theatre Royal* stood for another two weeks, it would have made history.)

On 9 January, a BBC Radio outside broadcast unit had planned to present the variety bill of that week, which would have been a first in Sheffield's history. Kemsley newspapers launched a subscription list for the artistes who had lost their costumes and props. The permanent theatre orchestra and Mr Can Castelli's band were also recompensed for their losses and given unemployment compensation.

Fortunately, there was neither injury or loss of life involved in the fire.

From 1927, the last theatre manager was Mr Arthur Holland, who, after the tortures of that awful night, was left sick at heart. To him it was like losing a friend. His office had gone but a box bearing his family crest had survived on top of the safe, unscorched and untouched. The motto was '*The Cross Rules the World*'. Strange, but true!

There is another story related by Tom Bolton, then licensee of the *Adelphi Hotel*. There was an 1869 *Theatre Royal* playbill in the pub and a few hours before closing time that night, its string snapped and it dropped to the floor. The name of the play was '*Act Drop*'! Coincidence or premonition?. Decide for yourself. However, Mrs Pat Crowther (nee Dawson), lived on Duke Street as a child, above her parents tobacconist's shop. That night, she awoke without reason and went to her parents rear bedroom and opened the curtains and saw the fierce blaze which tinged the night sky with crimson. In her case, a premonition which was fulfilled. Nearly £50,000 of damage was done to the theatre. The cause of the blaze remains a mystery. Another peculiar feature of the timing of the fire, was that on Sunday nights only, no duty fireman was present in the building and the theatre had not been used for over twenty eight hours before the fire was discovered.

After eventual clearance, the site was never developed, being used as a car park for many years. In 1970, it was partially excavated for the construction of the new *Crucible Theatre* and parts of the old *Theatre Royal* cellars were revealed. Today, the site forms part of the paved *Crucible* forecourt with grassed area adjoining and adjacent to the *Lyceum Theatre*.

Description of the building in 1935:

Altered several times and rebuilt in 1855 and 1901, the final façade facing the *Lyceum Theatre* was very imposing being built of red brick and trimmed stone adornments. To the right, a flat frontage with three large arched windows (two bricked up, the central having a glazed 'mullion' design) and above them seven tall arches, five being windows. In the centre window was the original 'Shakespeare' plaque and a smaller circular plaque on the wall at either side. Above was a tapered slate roof with three circular windows having stone 'scroll effect' trims. At street level were three sets of entrance doors, Circle, Stalls and Circle, Upper Circle, with a glass canopy above which covered the whole Tudor Street façade which extended round into Arundel Street, above the gallery entrance. (This having ten tall arched windows above and built in two linked sections at a lower level). In the canopy centre was a semicircular arch with '*Theatre Royal*' and adjoining ornamental lamps. At either end was a smaller triangular sign, also, similarly lettered.

To the left of the main façade was a lower level with six smaller arched windows. Viewed from the South East, the frontage had an elongated box roof with lower gabled roof below with a ventilation dome atop and the smaller stage roof behind that. There were four tall chimneys and a two level flat brick wall to the left of the Tudor Street façade which carried a billboard for both the *Lyceum Theatre* and the *Theatre Royal*.

THE HIPPODROME THEATRE
(Name derived from 'A circus for horse races')

Theatre of Varieties located at 34 Cambridge Street (formerly Coalpit Lane), also bounded by Wellington Street and Backfields. The architect was Bertie Crew (well known London Theatre Designer). The general Contractors were Messrs J. Parkinson and Son Limited. The capacity figures are as folows: 2730 (1910), 2445 (1935), 1419 (1960, the gallery in disuse).

The theatre proprietors were 'Hippodrome, Sheffield', but the presentations were under the control of Thomas Barrasford's Vaudeville Circuit. Before the theatre could be built, a 100ft chimney had to be demolished.

This massive hall was built to rival the mighty *Moss Empire*. The *Hippodrome* opened on 23 December 1907, making it the largest theatre in Sheffield, when the capacity was reputedly 4,000, but this would have included standees. its cantilever style of construction (no supporting pillars) was said to embody the longest circle girder ever used in a theatre. The theatre was declared open by Miss Elsie Savage, the daughter of a *Hippodrome Company* director.

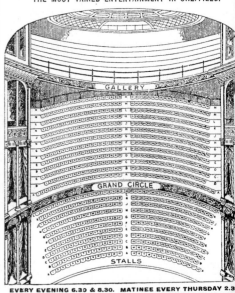

The opening presentation was a variety bill starring 'The Harmony Four', noted vocalists, supported by 'Davis and Gledhill', cycling troupes and 'Sisters Sprightly'. There was an interlude of 'Barrascope' topical films. On the opening night, the orchestra left much to be desired but thankfully, rapidly improved. Admission prices were from 3d to 1/6.

The early days were less than auspicious, however, business improved as the theatre became established and recognised for its quality programmes. Severe

Seating plan for the Hippodrome Theatre.

The Hippodrome Theatre, 34 Cambridge Street, 1963.

competition came from the *Grand* (West Bar) and the *Alhambra* (Attercliffe), who all presented variety programmes.

Externally the *Hippodrome* was a fine building. The frontage on Cambridge Street was executed in terracotta with granite pillars and marble enrichments. The central portico carried the name '*Hippodrome*', surrounded by designs depicting music, drama and art. The central section of the building was carried to a great height with windows and pilasters of Flemish renaissance style. The Wellington Street elevation incorporated two square towers with an intervening flat roof. The stage door and exits faced Backfields and Button Lane. Internally the auditorium was spacious, the walls embellished with arches, alcoves and pilasters in gold and white. Seating and draperies were of a plush crimson and the stalls and circle carpeting was green and grey. Spacious promenades surrounded the amphitheatre and circle whilst the proscenium was flanked by two enormous marble columns. The large stage extended to a depth of forty feet, reputedly it was the largest in Sheffield and one of the biggest in the north. its revolving stage once featured furiously galloping horses!

There were ten dressing rooms backstage. Wide marble stairs led to the foyer, which was designed in the style of a Venetian Palace with colonnades and alcoves adorned with marble pilasters and mirrors. The carpeting was of luxurious quality, the whole setting a very opulent tone.

In 1910, the seating was recorded as being 2,730: Stalls 370, Pit 800, Circle 520, Gallery 1000 and eight Boxes seating an additional 40. From 1907, it was the normal policy to show various short films in a variety bill, animated bioscope introducing films to audiences for forty one weeks, in 1908, thirty three weeks in 1909 and 'Barrascope', interludes shown for twenty weeks in 1910. Their frequency dwindled and was phased out after 1914. During 1912, Miss Annette Kellerman appeared. Then the current sensation, she was said to have 'the most perfect figure in the world'.

In 1913, '*Face to Face with Wild Animals*', starring Cherry Kearton was shown for two weeks at matinees and the film '*Through the Clouds*' was given very prominent billing, unusual in a variety show.

For programme information in 1917, you dialled 4110! '*Simba*' was presented in October 1929 and again in June 1930.

An unusual feature of the theatre was the sliding roof which 'sighed', open during the interval, enabling patrons to count the stars in the sky on fine evenings. It was also used on hot Summer days to keep the auditorium cool, being kept in use right up to the later years when '*Gone with the Wind*', starring Clark Gable and Vivien Leigh was shown. A fitting title for a breezy aid to patrons well being!

Various improvements were made to the theatre up to and including 1927, but it closed suddenly on 6 June 1931, during the movie boom, enabling a number of structural alterations to be carried out. A new projection box was constructed at the rear of the circle and Western Electric sound equipment and two 'Ross' projectors were installed. Some entrances and exits were altered and the auditorium was partially refurbished with new carpets, screen curtains, re-decoration and improved lighting system. The conversion was carried out by Associated British Cinemas Limited, who only leased the building but gained a 'shop window' in Sheffield. The *Hippodrome* opened as a cinema on Monday 20 July 1931, with *'Manslaughter'* starring Frederick March and Claudette Colbert. The supporting feature was *'Social Lion'* with Jack Oakie. Admission prices were: Stalls 1/-, Circle1/6d, Gallery 6d - before 4.00pm they were 1/- , 8d and 4d. Oddly for a cinema, the cheap seats were rear 'Gods'. Performances were continuous from early afternoon, this being the usual policy for city centre cinemas at the time.

The only new colour film of 1933 was *'The Mystery of the Wax Museum'*, which played the *Hippodrome* in September. In 1937, *'God's Country and the Woman'* was presented.

Little further alteration work was carried out until the theatre closed on 13 June 1938 for extensive improvement, including reseating and redecoration. It re-opened on 4 July 1938. There was some bomb damage on the first night of the blitz, Thursday 12 December 1940. The theatre was closed for repairs but soon reopened on 1 January 1941. There were occasional stage shows during the Second World War but they were few and far between.

When the lease expired in 1948, Associated British Cinemas, hesitated over its renewal and the theatre was promptly purchased by *The Tivoli*, (Sheffield) Ltd who quickly raised extra capital to complete the purchase. They were the former proprietors of the *New Tivoli*, Norfolk Street which had closed due to bomb damage. These premises are currently occupied by Swift and Goodison Ltd, undertakers.

The foyer was altered and improved, new Westrex sound equipment was installed in addition to 'Century', projector heads with 'Peerless' arc lamps.

The theatre reopened on 26 July 1948, with a revival called *'You were never Lovelier'*, starring Fred Astaire and Rita Hayworth. From this time, the management tried to promote certain programmes in unusual ways, one of which was when the BBC recorded audience gasps, during a matinee showing of *'The Unexpected'*.

A then current release, *'The Case of Charles Peace'* was accompanied by the Sheffield Photo Company's original 1915 film *'The Life of Charles Peace'*!

By 1953, not only Technicolor was well established, but the

Hippodrome also became the place for films in 3D, opening with 'Metroscopix'.

Films included, from 7 September 1953, '*Phantom of the Rue Morgue*', '*Kiss me Kate*', (June 1954), '*House of Wax*', (August 1954). This was the first major feature film shown in Sheffield to be projected in cinemascope. The panoramic screen was installed at the end of May 1954. The second Cinemascope presentation was '*In Command*', shown on 18 October 1954. The subtitled foreign film '*La Dolce Vita*', was shown in 1961.

The *Hippodrome* was the fourth Sheffield Hall to show films in Cinemascope, but was not yet equipped for stereophonic sound.

Music Hall at the theatre was a mere memory now but relics of the past still survived, including a gas lit gallery and chandeliers which had to be winched down from the ceiling for cleaning. As a cinema, The *Hippodrome* was rarely used for theatrical presentation though the licence was maintained. An unusual 'one off', was a series of plays presented by the 'Moral Re-armament Movement', from 7 May 1956. These were presented at two matinee performances and one evening show.

The stage was actually large enough to accommodate two battling armies in the *Hippodrome*'s last live presentation, a musical with a cast in excess of 200! As a theatre, the *Hippodrome* staged some of the biggest shows in Sheffield and many famous Music Hall artistes had performed there. Miss Ruby Johnson worked at the theatre for forty six years and recalled how in the early days, she sold chocolates from a silver tray. Uniform of those far off days, was black dress and hair bow with white apron.

Miss Gertie Gitana was once knocked over by the heavily fringed stage curtains whilst taking her bows!, while Miss Vesta Tilley 'the idol of the Halls', made her last ever theatre appearance at the *Hippodrome* and the audience stood ten deep!

Miss Marie Lloyd, Miss Hetty King, Mr Charlie Chaplin and Mr Max Miller all trod the boards at the *Hippodrome* theatre.

The biggest and most spectacular stage shows presented were '*Chu-Chin-Chow*', which ran for three weeks, direct from London and 'The Garden of Allah'.

Over the years, there were personal appearances of popular stars to promote their films. For example, in 1932, Leslie Fuller, star of many Elstree comedies and in 1946, William Hartnell, BBC's later television star as the first Doctor Who, was in the spotlight with '*Meet the Navy*'. In 1948 - William, '*Just William*', Graham and in 1953, Lisa Daniely and John Blythe '*Wedding of Lili Marlene*'. In 1957, there was a rare stage presentation '*Quartette*', featuring the music from the film '*The Tommy Steele Story*', which was the following week's main feature film.

Sunday opening was first permitted in 1944, though few Sheffield cinema proprietors showed any enthusiasm for the idea. Sailing in under the colours of ABC, the *Hippodrome* went into action on Sunday 20 August 1944. The Sunday programmes differed from the weekly ones, a virtually invariable policy, even when rival cinemas showed the same programme over seven days.

The gallery was now disused and by 20 December, 1959, only 913 Stalls and 506 Circle seats remained.

In 1954, the Manager, Mr Kirkham informed *The Star* newspaper that the theatre had been listed for compulsory purchase, at which time protests were made against the plan, but too late. The Compulsory Purchase was confirmed and as no appeal was negotiable, so purchase prices had to be discussed with the corporation. By this time, surveyors had already inspected the property. its fate was sealed when the *Tivoli (Sheffield) Limited*, was acquired by Garwood Investments Limited, a subsidiary of the developers Town and City Properties Limited.

By 26 November 1960, there were rumours that the *Hippodrome* had been sold for demolition. Mr Sidney Kirkham (Managing Director of *Tivoli, (Sheffield) Limited*, said that the rumours had no foundation. Adjoining properties were however being acquired by compulsory purchase, for the Moorhead redevelopment scheme and the future of the theatre looked grim.

It is interesting to record how the exterior of the *Hippodrome Theatre* looked at this time, being subjected to numerous alterations over the years.

This vast building consisted of an elongated frontage with box roof and a gabled section with a larger, higher stage section with a four sided box roof. Atop was a small ventilation structure, again with four sided roof and mushroom pot. A smaller gabled section adjoined the stage building to the rear, left and right. The frontage now sported a canopy over the entrance doors, under the central portico. The name '*Hippodrome*', was executed in slightly semi-circular lettering with Stalls and Circle in flat lettering to the left and right respectively. Billboards at either side end promoted the feature film presentation. For example '*Rebel Without a Cause*', starring James Dean, '*The Thousand Eyes of Dr Mabuse*' and '*The Greatest Show on Earth*'. Vertical *Hippodrome* signs were erected on the outer granite pillars facing up and down Cambridge Street. To the left was 'Oxleys' (gentlemen's outfitters) and to the right, 'Nell's', grill, snack and bar premises, both being a part of the main building at ground level. For many years a free house, 'Nell's' was displaying a 'Hammond Ales', sign right to the end. Its right side door had three left and two right boxed windows, with a central menu display at angles to the street. Naturally this cosy cafe was very popular with theatre-goers and the supper licence extended until 11.00pm. Adjoining was R.J. Stokes, paint and varnish shop and over the road in Wellington Street stood *The Barleycorn Hotel*, a public house which was very popular with servicemen during the Second World War. It still exists today as *Henry's Wine Bar*.

A uniformed usher in burgundy livery welcomed patrons to the theatre at opening times. Mr Charles Giles, now 89, had been commissionaire for forty one years. Cambridge Street bustled with activity at this time, with the queues entertained by street performers and *The Star*, vendors sold patrons their newspaper.

In about 1961, my parents, Mr and Mrs R.T. Hillerby recall seeing a stage presentation entitled '*The Park Drive Show*', sponsored by the Gallagher Tobacco Company who manufactured *Park Drive* cigarettes. The presentation starred Bill Maynard, and '*The Dallas Boys*'.

The end came swiftly for the *Hippodrome* and in 1962 this once grand theatre died with dignity.

The final film shown was chosen with great care since it had played the *Hippodrome* on no less than four previous occasions in, 1942, 1944, 1948 and 1952. Chief projectionist, George Clift and Manager, Mr R. Morris prepared for the final showing of '*Gone with the Wind*', which closed the theatre on Saturday 2 March 1962.

The prologue drifted across the screen to a hushed audience.

'*Once there was a land of Cavaliers and cotton fields, where gallantry had its last bow, where knights and fair ladies walked and chivalry ruled for a little spell, a civilisation gone with the wind*'.

Perhaps these words were the ideal choice to say goodbye to the one time magic that was the *Hippodrome*. A subdued, sad murmuring from a packed house prevailed, the mood fitted by the film's melancholy music. The radiators had warmed the theatre to a 'music hall fug' and some patrons took photographs.

Said one to a stranger, '*I courted here, as did my son, what will my grandson do now?*'. Backstage, the old dressing rooms were dim, quiet and holding their secrets. Way up in the roof, the abandoned Gods stared down on Circle and Stalls. Yet the benches were not empty, the ghosts and memories of fifty six years had shown them too much for that ever to be so. Retaining its spell to the end, it was still a proud theatre even as the speeches ended and the audiences filed out for the last time. The screen curtains closed for the last time and like the film presentation, the

Hippodrome was indeed soon 'gone with the wind'. Shortly afterwards it was demolished and the site was subsequently redeveloped.

The rear of the *Grosvenor House Hotel* now faces Cambridge Street above 'Sunwin Travel', 'Alliance and Leicester', 'Starworld' and a group of retail outlets front the site on three sides.

Notable Presentations: The *Hippodrome* presented plays and variety shows for more than twenty years, including:

Monday, 22 February 1909, the variety bill including 'The Stowe Brothers', novelty equilibrists, 'Jock Whiteford', the smart Scottish comedian, 'The Five Broadway Girls', vocalists and dancers and The Barrascope Animated Pictures. This was the name of an improved projector developed by Frank Backing and designed by Fred Borland, it was manufactured in Leeds. The programme featured a colour picture of the fox hunt entitled '*A Hunting Morning*'.

Monday 9 March 1909, the variety bill included: 'The Camplins', 'Madame Albani', the peerless 'Queen of Song' and 'Wright and Lawson'. The programme declared '*God Save the King*' and '*In the interest of public health, Jeyes disinfectants are exclusively used throughout this Theatre!*'. At the time, the productions had a paid matinee at 2.30pm.

Prices of admission were: Private Boxes 10/6, Orchestra Stalls 1/, Grand Circle 6d, Pit 4d and Gallery 2d. Early doors admission prices were a little higher, usually about 3d more.

Monday 22 December 1913, J.F. Elliton's grand Christmas pantomime was 'Mother Goose'. Matinees were on 26 December (Boxing Day) and Saturday 27 December. Children under twelve were admitted at half price.

In 1913, the theatre featured '*Little Lucy Linda*', the miniature Pavlova, in the pantomime '*Puss in Boots*'.

Monday 3 February 1913, featured Miss Florrie Forde, in her first twice nightly! Pantomime '*Bold Robin Hood*', or '*The Babes in the Wood*', produced by Gilbert Payne.

Saturday 5 December 1914, 'Matinee Performance' given by the *Hippodrome* proprietors in support of the *Sheffield Independent*, newspaper fund to provide Christmas Boxes for our 'Brave Boys on Land and Sea', at 2.30pm.

The manager at this time, Mr Walter Parham Wells.

Artistes included, 'Elsie Stead', character impressions, 'Joe and Willy', eccentric comedians from the '*Follies Bergere Paris*' and Phil Phills' coon delineator, by kind permission of the Rotherham *Hippodrome Theatre*.

24 December 1916, an exceptional Christmas attraction, the sketch '*Rule 19*', by the famous dramatist Sir Arthur Conan Doyle, was

presented for the very first time in Music Hall at the theatre.

Artistes included, 'Francis Gerrard', and 'Boyce and Maynard'.

Monday 23 November, The British National Opera Company, presented 'Aida', 'Hugh the Drover', by Ralph Vaughan Williams and the first performance in Sheffield of 'Coffee and Cupid', arranged from Bach's 'coffee cantata' and conducted by, Mr (later Sir), Malcolm Sargent!. In 1927, this company also presented on Monday 11 April 'The Marriage of Figaro', by Mozart and during that same week 'Othello' by Guiseppi Verdi and Rossini's 'The Barber of Seville'.

On 6 January 1928, Julian Wylie Productions presented 'Mother Goose' with Shaun Glenville in the title role. Miss Dorothy Ward (his wife) also appeared. She was a famous, thigh slapping principal boy in pantomimes. This was a £12,000! pantomime production from the London Hippodrome Theatre, in later years it became 'The Talk of the

Programme from March 1931, featuring Billy Bennett and the Seven Karolla Girls.

TELEPHONE   **HIPPODROME**   THEATRE OF
23311   Resident Manager - - W. B. GIBSON   VARIETIES

MONDAY, MARCH 23rd, 1931   And during the week
TWICE NIGHTLY at 6-30 & 8-40

1—Overture   ..   ..   Orchestra

ANNETTE presents
2—THE SEVEN KAROLLA GIRLS   Youth! Beauty! Ability!

3—DELVAINE'S MARIONETTES   England's Premier Puppets

The Argumentative Comedians—
4—WILL COLLINSON and ALFRED DEAN
     Will Argue about " George "

5—LILIAN GUNNS   The New and Unusual Comedienne

6—LOUIS, the Famous French Clown, assisted by ANNA & EMMIE
     In their Wonderful and Laughable Musical Act

7—Orchestral Interlude

ANNETTE presents
8—THE SEVEN KAROLLA GIRLS   Youth! Beauty! Ability!

9—J. J. WILD'S FAMOUS LANCASHIRE PLAYERS
     In " The Widow who would "
     An Original and Unrivalled Comedy Sketch

The Popular Comedian—
10—BILLY BENNETT   " Almost a Gentleman "

11—GIRLIE WATT and TONY WOOD
     The New Comedy Vaudevillians

12—SCOTT and WESTON
     A Clever Comedy Highland Musical Team

GRAND PIANO supplied by Messrs. WILSON PECK Ltd.

Town', with original cast members including Mr Fred Conquest as 'Priscilla', the giant goose! It featured wondrous scenes, dazzling effects, sparkling songs and gorgeous dresses. Performed once nightly at 7.15pm, this was the pantomime event of the season in Sheffield, surpassing many others.

Monday 17 May 1928, Macdonald and Young presented, from the *London Hippodrome*, a two act musical comedy '*Mercenary Mary*', with a grand piano supplied by Messrs. Wilson Peck Limited.

Monday 12 August 1929, Francis Laidler presented '*Billy Blue*', a new type of revue, starring Tom Newell.

Monday 30 September 1929, Macdonald and Young presented, from the Palace Theatre, London, 'Princess Charming', with Frances Wadell and Nancy Fraser.

Monday 4 August 1940, a variety bill including 'Cyril Shields', the wireless conjuror, 'Bennett and Williams', two jovial boys with their Phono-fiddles and Stainless Stephen, real name Arthur Clifford Baynes, who according to the programme '*will address his fellow rate-payers*'.

Monday 9 March 1930, Clayton and Hough presented a new musical play '*Barbed Wire*', with a company of sixty artistes and twenty four guardsmen and the full guards band!

Monday 24 November 1930, twice nightly variety with 'The Stephen Anderson Girls', the most versatile girls in Vaudeville, 'Bud Ritchie' conversational comedian and 'Chefalo', the master illusionist assisted by the 'Magda-Palermo Lilliputians!'

And finally, Monday 23 March 1931, a variety bill including 'Delvaine's Marionettes', England's premier puppets, 'J.J. Wilds' famous Lancashire players' in an unrivalled comedy sketch '*The Widow Who Would*'! and 'Billy Bennett' the popular comedian with '*Almost a Gentleman*', which takes us right up to the time when as previously stated, the *Hippodrome* became a cinema, ending its days as a true variety theatre.

The row of shops including the Starstore, which now stands on the site of the Hippodrome Theatre, photographed in 1999.

THE ALHAMBRA, PEOPLES AND ROYAL PRINCESS' THEATRE, ATTERCLIFFE

It would be remiss to omit from our recollection of the Sheffield Halls the suburb of Attercliffe which boasted a *Palace of Varieties* and *Theatre Royal*. Over fifty years ago, Attercliffe was a thriving, self-contained township occupied by a friendly, working class community.

Located on Attercliffe Road, approximately 350 yards from the Staniforth Road junction was The Alhambra, which had a seating capacity of 1,600 (1,200-1904, 1,000-1931, 970-1937)

Mr Frank MacNaughten invested £10,000, to build a hall in this densely populated suburb. In 1897 he formed the *Alhambra Theatre Company* with co-director Fred Lawton, a local solicitor, which commissioned the new hall to be built approximately two miles from the city centre.

Architects, G.D. Martin and A. Blomfield Jackson, ex business partner of the celebrated architect C.J. Phipps, of Bath, designed this decent sized structure. They had previously designed both, Her Majesty's and the Prince of Wales theatres, London.

It was constructed by George Longden and Son Limited, who built many of Sheffield's cinemas. The rambling façade utilised various materials, including glazed brick and terracotta faience at the base, with red brick on the front flanking the staircase towers at either side. Each had two sets of double doors, reached by steps. An off centre entrance doorway was topped by a plainly ornamented flat pediment. Above this were five tall arched windows crowned by five taller, similar windows, all of ordinary design. Ornamental stucco completed the whole effect in the centre. The general effect was 'castle-like', with a domed roof at the stage end. In later years, the sign 'Palace Theatre', was erected across the frontage between the window levels. This was a working class hall, known locally as the *East End Theatre*. Working in the shadow of the city centre *Empire Theatre*, the *Alhambra's* admission prices were half those of their competitors, however, the standards of presentation did not compare either. Even so, there was great rivalry between the two

The Palace Theatre, Attercliffe.
(Formerly the Alhambra Theatre)

The Palace Theatre, interior after
redecoration in Moorish style, for
cinema usage in 1931.

RE-OPENING OF **PALACE THEATRE,**
ATTERCLIFFE.

NEW HOME FOR ALL-TALKING PICTURES.

theatres. The acts engaged to play the *Empire* received the same remuneration if they played the *Alhambra* and the citizens of Attercliffe enjoyed high class performances at affordable prices!

These were: Orchestra Stalls 1/-, Stalls and Balcony 6d and Pit 3d.

Internally, the auditorium decorations were of Moorish style, reflecting the theatre's name. Here there was no ornamented fibrous plaster, no pediments and balustrades embellished in gleaming gilt, no cherubic murals in delicate cream and gold. This was a plain theatre with a balcony supported by steel pillars in the stalls. A main feature was the proscenium arch, which was curved rather than the usual square shape. In front of the stage was a superb act drop executed by Mr McCullock, the appointed scenic artist, depicting the *Alhambra Court*, Crystal Palace, London. The house was lit throughout by electricity.

The *Alhambra* opened as a variety theatre on 3 January 1898, at which time the Manager was Mr Arthur. At this time the hall naturally ran two houses a night variety bills. The opening presentation was '*Professor Leslie's Leaping Dogs*', with supporting acts. Unfortunately, the opening weeks attendances were poor. They improved with time but the *Alhambra* never achieved its hoped for success. The theatre was eventually sold to T. Allan Edwardes of Derby and managed for them by the Walker family. Initially Mr Walker senior, an architect, ran it but later his two sons, Arthur R. and D. Speed Walker took control. Eventually they also purchased the lease.

The theatre re-opened on 1 August 1907 and was renamed the '*Palace Theatre*', which ran as a Music Hall until early in 1913, when it was sold again to the Roberto Brothers with the lessee being the 'Raymond Animated Picture Company'. From then on it was known as the '*Picture Palace*', under which name it operated as a cinema until 1919, although variety returned during the 1920s.

The *Palace* became a full time cinema from 1931. The most remarkable feature at this time was the new atmospheric decoration plan. Specialist cinema design artist Mr Fred A. Foster, of Nottingham, created a scenic impression for the audience of looking out from an Indian or Arabian style building onto a surrounding panoramic scene of mosques and minarets. They were reflected in an azure blue sea lapping against a lush tropical beach festooned with exotic plants and majestic palms. A truly magnificent effect!

The newly renovated cinema's first presentation was '*Broadway Scandals*', after which the Hall featured double bill programmes with a wide variety of films. In 1936 the cinema closed for three months to allow the installation of a new projection box and Western Electric sound system, however, the cinema closed down on 17 July 1937, having staged the occasional variety bills and pantomimes. The last film presentation was '*Sweet Aloes*' starring Miss Kay Francis. The *Palace* returned to full time variety and Music Hall greatness during August that year and in later years enjoyed the benefits of the post war Music Hall boom. The theatre was on the number two circuit, the majority of the presentations being in revue form. Many of the variety acts were compiled by district theatrical agents and presented on shoestring budgets. A large proportion of the acts that appeared at the *Palace* were second rate and lived almost on the breadline! It was a training ground for prospective management employees and artistes, indeed a galaxy of budding stars appeared there over the years. The impressive list includes Mr Charles Chaplin in Fred Karno's 'Mumming Birds' troupe and during the theatre's heyday, countless others. These included, Miss Hylda Baker, Mr Dan Young, Mr Frank Randle, Mr Bud Flanagan, Mr Harry Secombe, Messrs George and Harry Formby and Messrs Max and Harry Nesbitt. Mr Sandy Powell launched his solo career at the *Palace* and Mr Bill Waddington (of *Coronation Street* fame in later years) appeared, billed then as 'Witty Willie from Lancashire'. Making many appearances there, he once presented his own pantomime as 'Simple Simon' in '*Babes in the Wood*'. In the 1940s, the musical director was Mr Frank Payne. In earlier days, this position was filled, by Mr Jack

The author with Miss Beryl Reid, who played the Attercliffe Palace. (Photograph taken in 1980)

Chard, a figure of some renown. Immaculate, in evening suit and white gloves, he insisted on a spotlight focused on the rostrum to make his own dramatic entrance. Mr (later Sir) George Robey played the *Palace* and Music Hall veteran Miss Ida Barr made her farewell appearance there aged eighty! A certain Miss Violet Pretty went on to Hollywood and found fame as Miss Anne Heywood! Indeed, the great and the small, they all played the *Palace Attercliffe*! Speciality acts included 'The Sphinx', 'Death Ray', 'Macnorton, The Human Aquarium' who swallowed and regurgitated live goldfish and frogs!, 'Pedro' and Mr Fred Atcher in '*The Living Shop Window Mannequin*'. The grimy stage caused dirt to mess up the acrobatic acts' costumes and tights, prompting the audience cat call of '*Look at tha mucky legs*!' The theatre's dressing rooms had badly fitting doors and resident mice, but of course all theatres played host to these rodents. Miss Beryl Reid, (1910-96) comedienne, once complained that a rat had found its way into her dressing room and eaten a pair of her best knickers! Also, whilst waiting in the wings to go on stage, Miss Reid was in conversation with a young lady who formed part of the acrobatic act 'The Australian Air Aces'. According to Miss Reid, the girl said '*I don't know how I'll get through the routine tonight, I'm absolutely shattered, I made a blancmange this morning*!' True or not its a good story, which makes you laugh. Which is what the golden days of variety at the Palace where all about.

Throughout the Second World War the *Palace* continued to present pantomimes and variety, despite the severe staff shortages resulting from so many of the country's artists being called up. One old trouper of a Manager posted the playbills, saw the house in at the box office, then led the orchestra playing the violin! He was a true Atterclevian, one of a distinct breed of this part of old Sheffield. A notable pantomime '*Aladdin*' was criticised because of its drab costumes and shabby old sets. At this time a very young Max Bygraves played Aladdin's washerwoman mother 'Widow Twankey' and at one point impersonated Alec Guiness (Well anything goes in pantomime, including the timeless tried and tested routines which originate from the *Drury Lane Theatre*, London, pantomimes of the early 1800s). The pantomime seasons at the *Palace* were always very popular, usually with a run of six different weekly presentations! Christmas would commence with '*Cinderella*', then possibly '*Dick Whittington*' followed by '*Aladdin*' and so forth until mid February! They were small scale family pantomimes made up of laughter from good clean fun. Around the city, one could often see the small display posters for them, conspicuous by their vibrancy! At full house performances, the 'packers', men who were employed to crowd in patrons, would fit in as many standing patrons as possible. A far cry from the strict and very necessary fire regulations of today's theatre.

Miss Patricia Dawson appeared at the *Palace* as the fairy in the pantomime '*Goldilocks and the Three Bears*' and again later in the Ernest Payne tour of '*Mother Goose*', in which production she played principal boy for the first time.

During 1946, the theatre was smartened up, though nothing too drastic due to the stringent management budget of a smaller theatre. The worn out stage curtains were replaced and the safety curtain cloth was repainted by the Stilwell Derby Company, with local retailers advertisements. Though of small outlay, these improvements were significant, though preserving the image of a local theatre. A reputation which the *Palace* bore with pride.

In the 1950s, the audiences began to wane due to the introduction of television. Attendances were poor with odd exceptions and so the *Palace* adopted a policy of occasional presentations, some by Mr Paul (Strip) Raymond. Notoriously having the word 'nude' in their titles, they tantalised the audiences with a promise of outrageous lewdness! In actual fact, they were quite modest, especially by today's standards and a nude sequence only occupied a very tiny section of any variety bill. Nonetheless, the performances were strictly monitored by the watch committee and the stage was dimly lit. The girls were forbidden to move even a 'pinkie' finger as they posed topless striking artistic poses, often of classical origin. For example, 'Eve' in the garden of Eden, Lady Godiva giving her all on a horse in the streets of Coventry or Greek goddesses with hand maidens in attendance. Sheffield, however, once boasted '*Britain's first moving nudes*' by putting the girls on a conveyor belt to carry them over the orchestra pit! This was the era of such saucy presentations as '*Nudes of the World*', '*We Never Clothed*', '*Halt, Who Goes Bare*', '*Bareskins and Blushes*', '*Grin and Bare It*', '*Evening Nudes*' and '*Strip Strip Hooray*'! Yet even these seemingly questionable presentations created their own legendary stars. The one and only Miss Phyllis Dixey (born Selina, Newport, 1914) enjoyed an illustrious career as a stripper, with an act of quality and elegance, always posing 'for art's sake'. She always maintained a deliciously refrained technique which produced a delectable air of innocence. In contrast, Miss Gypsy Rose Lee, a stripper in American Vaudeville, presented a frank air of naughtiness.

Phyllis Dixey played the *Palace* in 'Peek a Boo' in 1955, (the original theatre tour of 'Peek a Boo Again!' opened in July 1945) a celebrated and rather vulgar revue with which she toured extensively, despite the fact that she considered the *Palace* to be a 'scruffy little place on the outskirts of industrial Sheffield'. Billed as 'A stripper of finesse, the girl

Miss Phyliss Dixey.

The Lord Chamberlain banned', Phyllis used this as her introduction. Her opening number was dedicated to 'La Belle France'. The revue included such scenes as,'Can-Can', 'Dormitory', 'Ulysses and The Sirens', 'Living Contribution to Art', 'Confessions' and 'The Brides Dream' as a Finale. This was an elaborate presentation with Phyllis's 'Andreiva' dancers doing a ballet routine dressed as pink sugar bridesmaids, around a twelve foot tiered wedding cake and Phyllis herself as the blushing bride, in a see through wedding dress! To close this act, she tossed roses from her bouquet into the audience, and disrobed until she was left wearing nothing but her bridal veil!

One of her most popular routines was 'Aphrodite's Triumph over Psyche', which was typical of the various historical tableaux included in the stage shows. Phyliss Dixey introduced 'striptease' to Scandinavia and toured 'Peek a Boo' there and despite her reputation for an air of gentility and refinement, she bared her bosoms for her Scandinavian audiences in the 'Aphrodite' routine!

Like many of her successors, Phyllis teased and tantalised her way across two continents! In another revue, standing in concealing lighting, rain showered down on her through a 'ceiling' during a thunderstorm! At the end of the act, Phyllis said to the audience '*I am soaked to the skin*'! Reputedly she bared all but in fact wore a 'cache-sex', which was a four inch by three inch piece of sticking plaster in the appropriate place and 'liquid silk' body makeup. She originally posed as a statuesque lamp, complete with shade and in later years, manipulated ostrich feather fans or furs to literally strip-tease! In the theatre, she refused to let the stagehands stand in the wings watching during her act, so instead they watched from the stage 'flies' above! At the height of her career she presented high quality revues with entertaining supporting acts. Those who saw her perform recall '*It was always a good show*'. In the 1940s, Phyllis could occasionally be found slipping out of her feathers and fans, for the boys in battledress who greatly enjoyed her appearances. She was also one of London's post war attractions, especially at the *Whitehall Theatre* which she leased in 1940. Phyllis regarded stripping as an art form and seen by thousands in the non stop revues staged there during and immediately after the Second World War. She was hailed as a sensation after taking war time London by storm. Phyliss timed her act to perfection, leaving audiences spellbound. She did little more than move slightly to reveal a minute amount of bare flesh.

Phyllis Dixey was always popular with students when she played the *City Varieties Theatre*, Leeds and they used to throw pennies onto the stage during her act prompting the remark, '*Every little helps*'. Morecambe and Wise were once a supporting act on her bill, while at

Jane.

one time Charlie Chester had written some of her numbers. Phyllis was approximately 41 years old when she played the *Palace* at Attercliffe, and by 1958, aged 44, her figure was beginning to slip, but she was still on the theatrical treadmill. She made one film with Herbert Lom 'Dual Alibi', a circus melodrama in which he played twins. Phyllis was filming during the day and still doing the twice nightly stage act in her game little trouper tradition. Her last appearance was at the *Palace Theatre*, Burnley, on 19 April 1958, unhonoured and unsung. She was taken to court for bankruptcy, after which she worked as a cook for the Merrit family, and eventually died of cancer in 1964.

Jane, of the cartoon strip in the *Daily Mirror* newspaper, also put in an appearance with her daschund dog 'Fritzi'. She was nude but never rude and topped the Sheffield area Halls for three decades. The character was conceived as a cartoon strip by Mr Norman Pett, in 1932, entitled 'Jane, The Diary of a Bright Young Thing', modelled on his wife initially but later on Miss Chrystabel Leighton-Porter, (1919-) a sixteen year old strawberry blond. Her hour glass figure and sexy whisper projected an innocent sexiness that was to come to life as 'Jane'. The act was passed by the then Lord Chamberlain, Sir George H. Titman! Jane's agent was an ex dancer, Lew Grade, later Lord Grade of *Elstree Studios* and her act always topped the bill.

The stage act, produced by Lew Lake was as follows: Opening with a street scene, four 'newsboys' carried placards spelling out '*Jane, who the army, navy, air force etc. wants*'. Next was a setting akin to the *Mirror* newspaper strip with '*Jane, by Pett*' atop. There were three compartments, first a bedroom with Jane asleep then awakened by a uniformed maid to slip on a dressing gown and enter, secondly a bathroom. Here she pulled across a shower curtain and bathed in silhouette. Thirdly, a dressing room where the maid brushed Jane's hair and attired her in a fabulous evening dress, then handed Fritzi to her. Fritzi was perfectly trained and would 'freeze' on command. What a trooper. Jane then stepped out of the cartoon toward the footlights as shimmering curtains closed behind her illuminated only in silhouette, she then half spoke and sang '*I'm Jane, the model, that's plain, I can't sing, I can't even croon and the dog I fondle is also a model, you've seen in a popular strip cartoon*'. These lyrics were written by Mr Monty Crick who later found fame as Dan in '*The Archers*'. At the song's end, Jane invited the audience on a world trip or through the calendar months, utilising twelve colourful settings for her and the girls to sing and dance. During the second act which occasionally utilised, (a reworking of the Fred Karno sketch 'A night in an English music hall' and three first half supporting acts,) Fritzi used to pose on a yacht with cap at a rakish angle with his front paws on the wheel! The act concluded with Jane appearing in yet another sumptuous, stunning evening gown. Jane was the main rival to Miss Phyllis Dixey and like her, did not allow stage hands in the wings during her act. The backstage area was fiercely guarded by Jane's 'Auntie', an elderly ex dancer! Jane still enjoys a comfortable retirement in Brighton. Now eighty, she was interviewed on television in March 1999, she still looks lovely. Jane regularly stopped the show when on stage.

She made only one film, '*The Adventures of Jane*', which was released in 1949. Other similar presentations utilised exotic place names like Paris, '*Night life of Paris*', '*The spice of Paris*', which invited you to stroll around the sidewalks of the world's gayest city 'Paree', '*It Started in Paris*', with Jimmy Gay, Vivian Lee and the 'Paris Maids', 'French Capers', presented by Tallent Productions!, featured the music of gay Paree-Marcel's fashion salon and the famous 'Bal Tabarin' night club. (Stockings were by Kayser-Bondor and cigarettes by Abdulla). Ultimately the *Palace* theatre, like so many others, was severely affected by the advent of television transmission after the war. In addition there was large scale re-housing taking place and factory closures in Attercliffe, which sounded the death knell for the theatre. After much heart searching, Mr D. Speed Walker could not avoid the deteriorating situation and decided to close the theatre. On 1 July 1955, the curtain fell on the usual variety show, '*Strip, Sauce and Spice*'. The poet and historian, Sir John Betjeman, considered the *Palace* to be of great historical interest and was saddened to see it go. The theatre was subsequently demolished in 1962 and shops were later built on the site.

Site of the Palace Theatre, *photographed in 1999*

THE PEOPLES THEATRE

L ocated at the corner of Pinfold Lane (now Staniforth Road) and Attercliffe Road. The architects were Flockton, Gibbs and Flockton. The theatre had a capacity of 1,100 (1904), and 950 (1923). Run by Edwardes of Derby and presenting dramatic fare. An extremely plain red brick building externally.

Opening on 26 July 1896, the presentation was Mr Gifford's number one touring company in '*No cross, no Crown*', a suitable melodrama.

On 13 December 1897, it was re-named the *Theatre Royal*. From 9 February 1907, it ran mainly as a cinema. Proprietors in 1904 were the North of England Theatre Corporation. From 1923, it became part of MacNaughtens Vaudeville Circuit Limited, leased to manager Wilfred Bryan. The theatre introduced animated pictures in June 1926, also phonofilms and singing and dancing short talkies in 1927 (the era of the jazz singer). A B.T.H. sound system was installed during September 1929.

The theatre closed its doors on 17 June 1933 but upon demolition some of its external walls were retained in the construction of the *Regal Cinema* which opened on the theatre site on 14 October 1935.

THE ROYAL PRINCESS'S THEATRE

Little is known about this theatre located in Effingham Street, in the Attercliffe area, being beyond The Wicker and near to Saville Street. Circa 1848, the sole lessee, Harvey Teasdale, presented, on Friday evening 8 June, an assorted programme. '*Don Caesar de Bazan*' and a farce '*Make your Wills*'. On Saturday 9 June, there was a presentation of the historical drama, in three acts, '*The French Revolution*', or '*The Bleeding Rose of Normandy*'. The evening concluded with a farce '*The Spectre Bridegroom*' in which Mr Harvey Teasdale himself played the part of 'Dickory'. Doors opened at 7.00pm, with admission prices; Boxes 1/-, Pit 6d, Gallery 3d. Indeed this was almost the spectre theatre, since despite extensive investigation, no further trace can be made.

In 1854, actors and performers had to stage stunts to attract their audiences. Harvey Teasdale constructed a basket in which he sat, to be towed along the River Don by a number of ducks! Reputedly, this event was watched by 'thousands of spectators'.

Playbill, The Royal Princess's Theatre-Attercliffe.

THE PLAYHOUSE THEATRE

Located on Townhead Street. In 1919, St Philips Dramatic Society leader, Mr Herbert M. Prentice approached The YMCA, Oxford Street Settlement in Shipton Street for permission to perform plays in the Little Theatre, situated on the ground floor. Permission was duly given. Seating was cane chairs and forms. Capacity was 150. The stage was a simple platform two feet off the floor!

The first presentation was on 24 November 1919, being a play 'The Silver Box' by John Galswworthy, starring Rowland C. Moore (a name later linked to Sheffield Public Transport). They were successful and during 1920, the company advertised their productions and hired a director at an annual salary of £600. They became 'The Sheffield Repertory Company' and announced an ambitious first season of plays. Although sponsored by the Joseph Rowntree Trust, they had a serious financial struggle as all twelve plays lost money. Arnold Freeman launched a public appeal to raise funds, writing to the Bishop of Sheffield and George Bernard Shaw. There was little public support, and Shaw replied unfavourably saying 'You are worse than a company promoter, I never give my name to anything I am not working in'. Losses on further productions were noted but in February 1924, the company moved to the South Street Schoolroom, Eldon Street at a hire of £15 per week, including lighting. Small funds were raised for alterations and provision of a stage but enthusiasm abounded and on 23 January 1924, they opened with 'The Romantic Young Lady'.

Capacity here was: Saloon 240, Balcony 190. Admission prices were balcony 2/4d and 3/6d (cushions provided), saloon 8d and 1/2d.

Still in debt the company struggled on, hand to mouth. Reports indicated that the rival Sheffield Playgoers Society, were considering taking Moorhead premises for conversion into a *Repertory Theatre*, though the plan never materialised. However, it spurred on The Sheffield Repertory people, who raised funds by jumble sales, donation and subscription. The company almost had to be wound up but were given a new lease of life in November 1925, when a two year grant of £500

per year was provided by the Carnegie Trust. However, the schoolroom presented many difficulties, including a lack of atmosphere. Many restrictions including a portable stage, proscenium, inadequate dressing rooms and fire danger queries from the authorities meant that more suitable premises had to be acquired. The Victorian Comrades (Temperance) Hall in Townhead Street was suggested. Built in 1855 it had also been the British Legion Headquarters, but the move did not take place until 1928. The purchase price was £5,500.
Capacity: Saloon 319, Balcony 222.

The late Sir Donald Woolfit joined them in 1926 as one of two professional players. During a performance of 'The Ship', by St John Irvine, two patrons took offence at an actor saying 'God Almighty', but were removed from the theatre, still protesting, by Herbert Prentice and two strong men. This incident was wonderful press publicity. In April, Mr Prentice, the founder resigned.

More losses were made and the General Strike of 1926 affected all entertainments adversely.

A grand opening night on 3 September 1928, hailed the presentation of 'The Dover Road', Lilian Bayliss (of Old Vic Theatre, London fame) was present and this notable beginning fared well for the future. Townhead Street was the company's most permanent home but in 1933 the financial position, was still shaky and closure seemed imminent once more on 27 January 1934.

This was a bitter blow after all the years of hardship. Fortunately, several notables took an active interest to prevent this, including Alderman Fred Marshall, Lord Mayor of Sheffield who chaired a public fund raising meeting. Another Town Hall meeting on 18 April 1934 featured a lecture in favour of supporting the theatre, by James Agate, well known theatre critic. A large sum was raised and eventually the figure was well in excess of £1,500.

Arthur H. Williams was appointed business Manager in September and in true spirit of the new board, an executive committee was established consisting of Messrs J.P. Lamb, Eric N. Simmons and T. Alec Seed to carry out the day to day running of the theatre. This new regime executed a bold 'do or die scheme', with straightforward ideals for the public's theatrical benefit in The Playhouse News in February 1935. The stage was partly reconstructed and obstructing walls demolished. Plays were now presented in groups of four, two comedies, one serious and one 'highbrow'. Bookings could be made at Messrs. Wilson Peck's, Cockaynes and Atkinsons. Admission prices 9d, 1/3d and 2/6d. By 1938, all booking services concentrated at the theatre. The summer season of 1935, ended with an original revue, 'The Forgotten City', written by board members and associates. The weather was intensely hot with the audiences sweltering throughout!

In 1936, St John Irvine, lecturer, attended a repertory performance and remarked upon the theatre's unprepossessing exterior, saying '*Every sign of neglect and incompetence! A typical Repertory Theatre*'. Many rapid changes were taking place and (Sir) Bernard Miles (founder of the *Mermaid Theatre*, London), joined the company as scenic designer for 'Vic-Versa', thus commencing his acting career in Sheffield.

In February 1938, it was considered that the name *The Repertory Theatre* was too up market and indicated amateur status and it was changed to *The Playhouse*. Geoffrey Ost, formerly of the *Buxton Opera House*, was appointed producer from April and became resident director for twenty six years. In his first year, (Sir) Alec Guinness appeared at *The Playhouse* for two weeks, giving an outstanding performance in William Shakespeare's '*Macbeth*'. During the war years, the company moved to *The Little Theatre*, Southport when the compulsory closure of city theatres was enforced as a result of the threat of bombing. Just before the declaration of war in September 1939, a new switchboard, big enough to serve a new theatre, if built, was installed and plans were being considered to reconstruct the theatre.

Architects, Hadfield, Cawkwell and Davison were to execute a three-phase plan at a cost of £11,000 for frontage, stage and single slope auditorium. A new building elsewhere in the city was also a proposition discussed, however, they were all brought to nought by the outbreak of the Second World War.

Management costs, even with the theatre closed were very high but the 'phoney war', period eased the tension and with a growing public demand for the *Sheffield Playhouse* to re-open became too insistent to ignore. This was done and no doubt the Southport venture helped for it enabled the company to recover losses and achieve a sound financial position.

The Playhouse re-opened on 26 November 1939 with '*The Last of Mrs Cheney*', the new producer being Robert Lees. Performances were twice nightly. Initially patrons braved the blackout but admissions dwindled and early in 1940, the board realised that the re-opening was a financial mistake and in April, the theatre closed again and was let to the Brightside and Carbrook Co-operative, for use as a store.

Not until late August 1944, did the board consider re-opening the theatre, as bombing of northern cities had slackened, hopefully on a permanent basis. The building had also in recent times been let as a dance hall and was in a shocking state. Seating and scenery required renewal, the building needed cleaning up and decorating, plus electrical

The interior of Sheffield Repertory Theatre, during redecoration in 1945.

restoration work was necessary. The balcony was re-floored and original cinema projection box removed. The entire auditorium was re-painted since materials were by then more readily available. *The Playhouse* re-opened on 24 February 1945, with 'The Peaceful Inn', and all presentations now ran for two weeks. This successful policy doubled the attendance of Repertory audiences. The players, again under H.M. Prentice formed a good team. Mrs Meeke and Mrs Angus ran the Box Office. Mrs Gladys Watts was caretaker throughout the war. During the awful night of 12 December 1940, when the city was dreadfully damaged by bombing, *The Playhouse* roof was lifted by the blast but luckily dropped back into place. Mrs Watts spent most of the night moving wines and spirits to the safety of the cellar, partaking of a small whisky for good measure, which she subsequently offered to pay for!

In July 1949, Mr Patrick McGoohan joined the company as assistant stage manager. He was a former light-heavyweight champion boxer in Sheffield. (In later years he starred on television in 'Danger Man' and 'The Prisoner').

A radio broadcast was made about the theatre in March 1949

Exterior view, Sheffield Repertory Theatre, Townhead Street, 1945.

featuring Mr T. Alec Seed speaking on '*The History of the Company*'. Reference is made later to actors who have since become famous, following their modest beginnings with The Playhouse theatre. In 1951, the company was flourishing with well-produced plays and once again the board considered reconstruction of the building. The single exit balcony, could have adversely affected the annual licence renewal, so investigations were made regarding refurbishment. Architect, Robert Cawkwell produced plans for a three part reconstruction: stage, auditorium and amenities, i.e. cafe, bar, booking hall, etc. However, the estimated costs were too high and the board considered the problems of funding and revenue losses whilst the theatre was necessarily closed.

However, matters came to a head following a structural examination, after which the ceiling was declared unsafe, meaning no licence renewal. A stay of execution was granted to replace it, but this in turn would affect the stage and auditorium. Despite licence problems and a building materials shortage, the plans were submitted on 9 June 1952.

Divided as follows: New ceiling, new fire curtain with consequent stage and proscenium alterations, auditorium and circle modifications and renovation of cafe, bar, toilets and entrance hall. Estimated renovation costs amounted to £20,000. The theatre closed in 1953 and the company transferred to the *Library Theatre*, Norfolk Street on 4 May. Sir Stuart Goodwin gave a generous donation towards the costs. Premises also had to be taken in Fentonville Street to store the accumulated stock of scenery and properties, valued at some £3,000. A £750 grant was made from the Arts Council for the fire curtain with a gift of a further £500 from the city trustees. Eventually, the new theatre was completed at a final cost of £41,000. The re-opening presentation was 'The Young Elizabeth', performed before an invited audience including Alderman J H Bingham (Lord Mayor), Master and Mistress Cutler, University representatives, church, legal and social dignitaries and representatives of the craftsmen who had worked on the restoration project. At the time of opening, the attendances were excellent and an 80 per cent permanent booking figure was maintained for many years. The building debt was virtually repaid within one year of opening. A carved plaque, in sycamore, to commemorate the benefactors of *The Playhouse*, was placed over the internal entrance doors and unveiled on 2 September 1957, by Alderman A. Ballard (Lord Mayor). The wording was,

The proscenium and stage of the Repertory Theatre *in 1945.*

'The re-building of this theatre in 1953 was made possible by the generosity of Sir Stuart and Lady Goodwin, the Arts Council of Great Britain, The Sheffield Town Trustees and all those who for over thirty years have supported the repertory movement in Sheffield'.

Despite increasing costs and difficulties over the selection of plays and players, success continued and was consolidated. New plays were produced for the first time on any stage and during September 1958, a new play *'Reward in Heaven'*, by former actor Roger Milner, was produced. This was in celebration of fifty years of the repertory movement founded by Miss Horniman in Manchester. The theatre's success depended on good management, choice of plays, audience comfort and chiefly on the popularity of the productions presented.

The company was now wholly professional and high production standards firmly established the *Sheffield Playhouse* in public affections.

In 1965, Colin George took over as Director and that year he presented the finest season in the history of the *Playhouse* including *'Twelfth Night'*, *'Inadmissible Evidence'*, *'The Bald Prima Donna'*, and *'The Importance of being Earnest'*, which was presented from 3 May 1966. The theatre's biggest success came on Monday 29 August 1966, when *'The Stirrings in Sheffield on a Saturday Night'*, was presented. Based on the outrages of the 1860s and the disturbances which centred around the Sheffield cutlery grinders, it was presented again from Wednesday 27 November 1968.

Some of the plays presented in the 1960s were by Brecht, John Osbourne's *'Look back in Anger'*, and *'The Ruling Class'*. These modern plays did not appeal to some older members of the audiences and there were walk-outs. However, they brought about a break-through with the younger generation. (Myself included - see footnote).

Modern presentations included, Monday 4 December 1961, *'Celebration'*, by Keith Waterhouse and Willis Hall; 20 November 1961, *'Mandragola'*; Tuesday 18 July 1967, in repertoire, *'Ring O' Roses'* (the great London plague in Eyam of 1865/6). 2 October 1968 *'The Comedy of Errors'*; 23 October 1968, *'Who's Afraid of Virginia Woolf?'* The final production at Townhead Street was during May 1971 *'Britannia's Boys'*,

The *Playhouse* closed in June and was sold in 1973 for £63,000 to a property developer. The company then moved to the newly built Crucible Theatre, Tudor Square which was their new home in which they continued to achieve success under the guidance of director Colin George. The proceeds of the Playhouse sale contributed towards the Crucible's building costs.

Exterior view, the new Sheffield Playhouse, mid 1960's

Footnote:

It was my visits to the Playhouse in the mid 1960s which fuelled my developing passion for the theatre. I was so lucky to see such excellent productions as 'The Knack (1966), 'Rattle of a Simple Man', 'Where are you going now Then?', 'The Duchess of Malfi' (1968), 'The Stirrings in

Interior of the new Sheffield Playhouse.

Sheffield' (with David Bradley and Dorothy Vernon) and 'Listen for the Trains, Love' with Jeff Rawle in 1968.

Being a teenager then, to be exposed to such varied, powerful and sometimes shocking drama was a fantastically exciting experience. I can recall that admission on a Saturday matinee was 3/6d! Sweet old dears sold you a programme priced 6d and a cup of tea cost - well I can't quite recall. I do remember that the forthcoming productions were projected onto the fire curtain in the interval, spotlight beams crossing right over left to form the whole in the centre by Stillwell- Derby. My good friend Richard L Roper and I spent many happy hours in this lovely, intimate little theatre which had a look and smell of faded elegance, but it was real theatre. The Playhouse was a nursery for some of the most illustrious actors who appeared in repertory: Margaret Tyzack, 5.9.35, Rachel Gurney, 1943, Patrick McNee, 1948, Peter Sallis, 10.7.50. Peter Barkworth, 1950, Frank Thornton, 1951, Paul Eddington, 21.1.52, Wilfred Bramble, 1955, Keith Barron, 1.9.56, Anne Stallybrass, 24.7.62, John Noakes, 29.1.62, Jane Rossington, 1.4.64, Peter Baldwin and Zibba Mays, 15.8.66, Jeff Rawle, 18.8.69, Nigel Hawthorne, 9.2.70,

Programmes, 'The Stirrings in Sheffield', 1968 and 'Listen for the Trains, Love', 1968.

Gorden Kaye, 3.8.70, Robin Nedwell, 5.4.71 and Duncan Preston. Lally Bowers was in the 1938/9 company and Ella Atkinson is very well remembered as a stalwart member of the repertory company. Joining in 1931, she appeared in 200 productions and last appeared at the Crucible in 1974. Her debut was in 'The White Headed Boy', with Sir Bernard Miles (1907-1999) and Laurie Lingard, on 8 September 1924. Her last appearance at the Playhouse was in 1971, in 'The Father' by Strindberg. She gave many fine character interpretations in a long, rewarding career. Aged 88 she passed away on 3 July 1992.

Ruth Robinson was the first professional player. Notable productions being: 'Gigi' 13.4.59, 'The Boy Friend' 23.4.63, 'A Kind of Loving' 29.3.66, with Dorothy Vernon, Chris Wilkinson and Ella Atkinson - a kitchen sink drama set in Cressley, South Yorkshire. 'Juno and the Paycock' 11.4.66, 'A Flea in her Ear' 15.4.66, 'Charley's Aunt' 30.8.65, 'Hamlet' 14.10.65, 'Comedy of Errors' 2.10.68, 'The Matchmaker'

21.5.69, 'Charlie Peace' 16.7.69, (noted Sheffield villain) and Dame Edith Evans - 'Reading for Pleasure' in 1969.

At Christmas times, over the years, 'Toad of Toad Hall' was very popular being presented at least three times; 31 December 1932, 27 December 1948 and 24 January 1949, each time running for two weeks. The early Christmas shows were very popular since local children were recruited from local dance schools, etc. Parents helped out too. Mothers in dressing rooms and fathers manning the auditorium doors. Traditionally, a party was held between the last matinee and evening performance which was always thoroughly enjoyed by all.

Specifications of Renovation 1953:
Now seating 547 people in stalls and circle.
Backstage and dressing room areas unchanged.
Stage dimensions; stage to fly 19'6' - to grid 39'. Flyrail to grid 36'.
Proscenium opening 26'; Wing opening 28', stage footlights to back wall 18'.

Site of Sheffield Playhouse, *photographed in 1999.*

Act VII – Reprise

THE LYCEUM THEATRE

❧

Good times and bad times,
I've seen them all
but my dear, I'm still here
(from '*Follies*' by Stephen Sondheim)

L ocated on the corner of Arundel and Tudor Streets. (Originally Talbot Street). Designed by the Architect William J Sprague, it had a seating capacity of 3,000. The site of this theatre had a very chequered history, firstly accommodating Tudor House and gardens and later an Artillery Depot. Leno's Circus of Varieties followed, it was here that Dan Leno's father judged clog dancing contests.

The theatre was built in 1879, as *Hangler's Circus*, it was later known as *Alexander Stacey's*, then theatre. This wooden structure was destroyed by fire in May 1893 and was later rebuilt as the *City Theatre*, by architects Walter Emden and Edward Holmes. It opened on 26 December 1896 with '*A Royal Divorce*'.

This structure too was partially destroyed by fire during the winter of 1896 and the building changed hands into the ownership of Mr John Hart in January 1897. He engaged the famous theatre architect of the day, Mr W. G. R. Sprague, to rebuild the ravaged

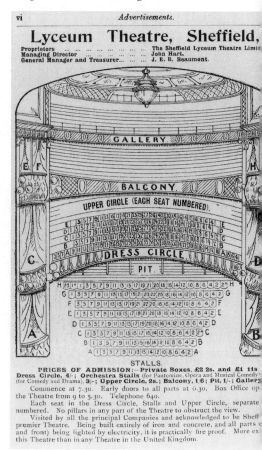

The Lyceum Theatre seating plan.

The Lyceum Theatre, Tudor Street and Theatre Royal opposite.

Mr Michael Dennison and Miss Dulcie Gray, Lyceum appeal, 1969.

Dame Anna Neagle.

auditorium and in collaboration with Edward Holmes, he redesigned the Circle, Gallery, Boxes and front of house areas. A blending of styles gave a pleasing whole, since he had a magnificent flair for theatrical atmosphere, transforming it into the handsome and newly named, *Lyceum Theatre*. (The name *Lyceum* means a large public building, or from the Latin - a garden near the temple of Apollo where Aristotle taught). The theatre is now thought to be the only surviving provincial theatre designed by William Sprague.

The auditorium had an opulent air of elegance with its beautiful Louis Quatorse plasterwork in gilt and cream finish. There were handsome representations of fine art on painted panels between chubby plaster

Mr John Hanson, star of Student Prince' and 'The D Song', the most famous shadow of them all.

cherubs, all of which overlooked luxurious carpeting and red plush seats from on high. Elegance was the keyword throughout and the balcony was one of the earliest examples of a cantilevered construction in the provinces. The proscenium arch was a frame of riotous Rococo openwork, being a plasterwork vallance covered in gilt and set against the backdrop of a crimson velvet curtain. An elaborate gas lighting system picked out the stairways and the auditorium was illuminated by electroliers above the square, fluted cornered dome. All of which shone down upon the luxurious establishment that the *Lyceum* had now become. Retiring rooms in each section of the theatre were decorated with Japanese wallpapers and adorned with richly framed mirrors. The theatre exterior was a bold and striking classical design with a 70ft high circular domed tower to the left elevation with a 12ft high flying figure of Apollo atop. A handsome iron and glass canopy above the corner entrance doors and the facade had a stucco covering overall, relieved with foliage and flowers. It is believed that the *Lyceum* had more entrance and exit doors than any other theatre in the country at the time.

The main façade had Greco Ionic pillars dividing a double row of windows above a central exit door with flanking pillars and ornamental pediments. The top windows were surmounted with semi circular arches with swirling stucco relief. The whole was relieved with terracotta and cream stonework. Above these at roof level were balustrades and decorative urns. (During the Second World War, these urns and the

The Lyceum Theatre, side elevation, 1964.

Apollo statue were removed to prevent damage from their possible falling during air raids. They were never seen again until 1990.

Opening night was 11 October 1897 when the Carl Rosa Grand Opera Co. took the stage with Bizet's opera 'Carmen'. The theatre attracted many of the great artistes of the day including Sir Henry Irving and Miss Ellen Terry the following week. (Irving made his farewell visit to the *Lyceum* in 1905 and he died at the Bradford *Alhambra* the following week).

'*Sweet Nell of Old Drury*': A play about King Charles II and his mistress Nell Gwynn, toured to the *Lyceum* after playing the *Theatre Royal*, Bournemouth.

There was a backstage fire in 1899, which destroyed the stage and dressing rooms. Only the safety curtain saved the auditorium. Following rebuilding and renovation, the theatre re-opened on 26 December with the pantomime '*Twinkle little Star*'.

The great Anna Pavlova appeared in 1912, while Mr Jack Buchanan appeared in 1916 with '*Tonight's the Night*'.

Miss Sybil Thorndike appeared

The Lyceum Theatre, August 1964.

in 1923 in '*The Scandal*', and Miss Evelyn Laye appeared with Mr George Graves in 'The Merry Widow' in 1923. Mr Ivor Novello played the *Lyceum* in 1931 with '*The Truth Game*'.

Dame Anna Neagle, (1904 - 1986), appeared in September 1960 in '*The More the Merrier*', July 1961 in '*Nothing is Free*', and in December 1963 in '*Person Unknown*'. (In the 1980s I met Dame Anna at the *Grand Theatre* Leeds, where she was starring as 'Mrs Higgins' in the Cameron Mackintosh tour of '*My Fair Lady*', with Miss Liz Robertson as '*Eliza*'. She was the charming first lady of the theatre and one of the last truly great stars. We maintained contact as friends, until her death in 1986.)

It was at the *Lyceum Theatre* where I first fell in love with the stage and became totally caught, on the hook of its magic spell. In August 1964,

Mr John Hanson appeared at the *Lyceum* in '*The Maid of the Mountains*', and again in August 1965 in '*The World and Music of Ivor Novello*, with Miss Jean Bayless. (She was the original 'Maria' in '*The Sound of Music*' at the *Palace Theatre* London in 1965).

Even the famous '*Black and White Minstrels*', made two visits to the theatre in 1964 and 1965.

In my early teenage visits to the theatre, I saw Mr Michael Dennison and Miss Dulcie Gray in '*On Approval*' in November 1966, Mr Nicholas Parsons and Miss Prunella Scales in '*Say Who You Are*' in February 1967, Miss Celia Johnson and Mr Michael Hordon in '*Relatively Speaking*' in March 1967 and Mr Robertson Hare, whose catchphrase was 'Charge', in '*Arsenic and Old Lace*' on 27 March 1967. Mr Jeremy

The interior of the Lyceum Theatre, in the mid 1960's.

Hawk in 'Jane Eyre' in March 1967 and Mr David Kossof and Miss Helen Shapiro in 'Never Too Late' during April 1968.

Croft House Amateur Operatic Society presented '*The King and I*' during April 1966, '*The Lisbon Story*' in April 1967, for two weeks and '*Robert and Elizabeth*' from 19 March 1968. This production featured the original sets and costumes from the *Lyric Theatre*, London, which starred Miss June Bronhill and Mr Keith Michell.

From 11 March 1968, Sheffield Amateur Operatic Society presented the Yorkshire West Riding premiere of '*Camelot*', their 50th anniversary production, which featured costumes from the *Drury Lane Theatre*, London, production. Mr Keith White played King Arthur and Miss Pauline Coopland the Lady Guinivere.

They presented Ivor Novello's '*Perchance to Dream*', from 3 March 1969 This celebrated and haunting musical is set in a house called 'Huntersmoon', and featured the beautiful song '*We'll Gather Lilacs*'.

Sheffield Teachers presented 'Orpheus in the Underworld' in November that same year. I can clearly recall seeing the D'Oyly Carte Opera Co. in '*The Pirates of Penzance*', '*The Mikado*' and '*The Gondoliers*' in March 1969.

This was their last visit to the *Lyceum* theatre prior to its closure. Sheffield born Mr Kenneth Sandford appeared in these excellent productions with Mr John Reid. (The D'Oyly Carte first visited the *Lyceum* in October 1898. Previous visits to Sheffield always saw them at the *Theatre Royal*).

The Autumn season of 1968 had re-opened with Robin Hall and Jimmy MacGregor in the '*White Heather Club*', from BBC Television.

Elmsdale Amateur Operatic Society presented '*My Fair Lady*' from 11 November for two weeks.

Like so many others, I remember as if they were yesterday instead of thirty years ago. I have particularly fond memories of two *Lyceum* pantomimes which I was taken to as a treat on New Years Day. In 1960 John Beaumont presented '*Puss in Boots*', with Arthur Haynes and Freddie Sales (Frederick Harry Walker, 1920-95) as the Dame. I can vividly remember going up on stage and doing the song sheet with the other children and shall never forget the brilliant light, heavy greasepaint and that marvellous applause!

In 1966 the pantomime was '*Cinderella*', starring Dickie Valentine, Cardew Robinson (real name Douglas Robinson, 1917-93), Joe Black and Miss Wendy Wayne. This was a lovely old traditional Howard and Wyndham pantomime which I enjoyed so much I confess I saw it at least four times during its run. I first met my good friend Wendy Wayne that year, in a little papershop, now long demolished, on Tudor Street. She

Singer Dickie Valentine and the ladies of the chorus, 'Cinderella' 1966.

became engaged to Dickie Valentine and the local papers declared 'Buttons to Marry His Cinders!', which he did the following year, 1967, when Wendy returned to Sheffield to play 'Polly Perkins' in 'Robinson Crusoe'. Freddie Frinton also starred doing his famous drunk sketch 'Dinner for One', with Kathleen West. (This was a masterpiece which I was priveledged to witness).

The last pantomime at the *Lyceum* was in 1968. This was 'Dick Whittington' with Vince Hill and comedienne Dorothy 'Dottie' Wayne, (1936-) the famous whistler and comedienne.

Alan Curtis spent 26 weeks of 1954 at the theatre as leading man with Harry

Mr and Mrs Dickie Valentine (actress Wendy Wayne), 1968.

Hanson's 'Court Players', featuring a different play each week. Everything from '*The Age of Consent*', to '*The Gay Bachelor*' and as the lead in Bram Stoker's '*Dracula*'.

A more famous '*Dracula*' appeared in 1951, in the form of the legendary American Film star Mr Bela Lugosi, who appeared regularly in a green mist!

Indeed, the *Lyceum* saw them all, including Morecambe and Wise, (John Eric Bartholomew 1926-1984 and Ernest Wiseman, 1925-1999) who appeared in two 1950s pantomimes.

Musical Extravaganzas, opera, ballet, comedy and tragedy. Drama and pantomime, were all on the bill of fare. The *Lyceum* was somewhat grander than the *Empire*, even to the selling of expensive chocolates and ice cream tubs in the intervals by attendants. The theatre was refurbished in July 1936, with new heating, lighting and recovered seats. Prior to Christmas 1939, the ground floor was recarpeted and reseated. Entrances to the stalls and new bars at this level were constructed, removing the necessity to climb stairs to circle level in order to gain access to the stalls.

During 1943 the Lyceum was closed for a complete interior transformation with redecoration in shades of beige, french pink, coral green and rose. New stage and auditorium curtains of crimson were also installed.

Mr Vince Hill, 'Dick Whittington', Lyceum Theatre 1968.

Outside on the circular entrance tower, beneath the dome, the name 'LYCEUM', was executed in large glowing neon letters.

A counterweight system was installed on the stage during November 1956. Under investment and lack of refurbishment in the 1960s led the theatre into a steady decline up to the point of closure in 1969.

By March of that year, history had passed the *Lyceum* by and it became a temple to bingo, from April 1969 until March 1972. Back in the 1967 season, there had been bingo on the stage in an attempt to make the theatre pay. Cries of 'House' replaced audience applause and the cherubs gazed 'eyes down', in mute disapproval.

Planners and Councillors squabbled over the site and dry rot took hold of the faded and neglected auditorium with its leaking roof.

In May 1969, a 'Save the Lyceum' campaign was launched with support from Michael Dennison and Miss Dulcie Gray. (Miss Gray recalled appearing years before at the *Lyceum*, when there was a terrible smell in her dressing room. On investigation the cause was found to be a dead rat behind the sofa! Her husband Mr Dennison resumed his theatrical career at the *Lyceum* following wartime military service, in the play '*Eve in Paradise*'. Mr Jimmy Jewel also pitched in on the 'Save the Lyceum' project, but in the meantime, the Manager Mr John Beaumont had applied for a full time bingo licence.

In the face of pressure for demolition, the building was declared a Grade II listed building in March 1972. This primarily due to the fine internal plasterwork and proscenium arch, rather than the exterior, which by then had lost all its embellishments and was flat, drab and not a little shabby.

In April 1975, *The Lyceum Trust* was formed, but by now the theatre was crumbling into ruin and a property company retained by the trust, failed to take it over because of non theatre usage plans. The building was sold to George Webster and Kevin Johnson, who reopened it as a rock venue from July to October 1981. They spent £250,000 on renovations to the building, repainting the exterior, though violating it with the inclusion of a shop unit. They also repainted the interior in two shades of ivory and red. All the seats in the stalls were also removed.

In January 1985, Academy Enterprises of Bournemouth came along with a plan to rename the theatre '*The Academy Disco and Restaurant*'.

These schemes foundered over licencing objections, but the building was put in mothballs while restoration plans were prepared by David

Heigh and Norman White, of South Yorkshire Opera. With support from the Royal Bank of Scotland and Sheffield City Council, they purchased the *Lyceum* and then realised the enormity of what they had involved themselves in. A new trust was formed and restoration costs were estimated as being approximately three million pounds!

Work was carried out to make the building waterproof, but it was soon realised that the *Crucible* and *Lyceum* trusts would have to unite, which they did in January 1989.

In December, four million pounds

The Lyceum Theatre, interior after redecoration as a rock concert venue, 1981.

Author with Mr Keith Barron, Lyceum Appeal, 1980's.

was given by the European Regional Development Fund, towards the rebuilding project. It actually cost twelve million pounds to restore the *Lyceum* to its current delightful condition. Thanks to the efforts of the architects, Renton, Howard, Wood and Levin, the auditorium is virtually an exact replica of the original three tier design with horseshoe shape and seating for 1130 people.

The extended stage with new tower is one of the deepest in Britain. Modern dressing rooms and backstage facilities now exist, while original

The Lyceum during internal reconstruction and renewal, preserving its Victorian heart, 1989. Courtesy of E. Lawrence/Peter Johnson, PMC Communications Ltd.

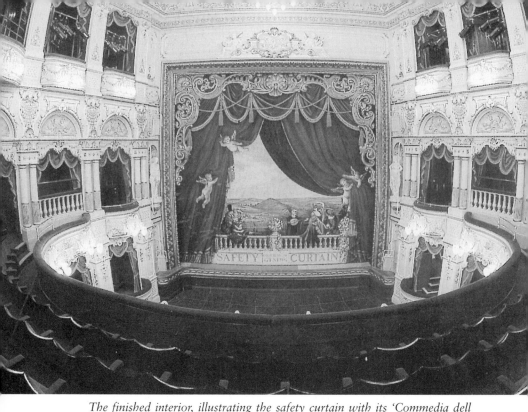

The finished interior, illustrating the safety curtain with its 'Commedia dell 'arte' design, December 1990.

The Lyceum in 1999, almost totally restored to the original design, with the exception of a new side ornamental canopy.

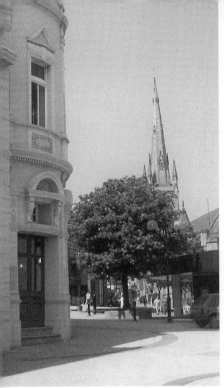

Lyceum Theatre and site of Theatre Royal, 1999.

A 1940's couple outside the Lyceum? Actually Glen and Melanie Sanderson, 1999!

mouldings, paint and gold leaf samples were taken in order to faithfully reproduce the original interior of the auditorium. New crimson curtains with gold braids, red seat covers and red painted rear walls, enhance the ivory and gold colour scheme.

The *Lyceum* was once a lost theatre, but it has been saved for the city and the nation.

In the words of Cole Porter, '*Another o'pnin, Another Show*'.

The curtain went up again on a new era in December 1990, when Mr Paul Nicholas starred in the Joseph Papp Broadway production of '*The Pirates of Penzance*'. Mr Danny La Rue appeared in the pantomime '*Aladdin*', as 'Widow Twankey' in 1996, and the theatre continues to present top drama, opera, ballet and musicals.

Author with Paul Nicholas, who re-opened the Lyceum with 'The Pirates of Penzance' on December 10, 1990.

Finale

IN CONCLUSION

Τhe halcyon days of the variety theatres are now little more than fond memories. With them went the iniquitous dens of the Music Halls (in 1868 the era Almanac listed ten) and the dream Palaces such as the Empire, Theatre Royal and adventurous Playhouse. We can record facts, figures and dates, but cannot preserve the smells, sound and atmosphere that were an essential element in the theatres of yesteryear. To quote the words of Dorothy Reynolds and Julian Slade in the musical 'Salad Days':

> *'If I start looking behind me and start retracing my track, I'll remind you to remind me we said we wouldn't look back'.*

But we did,...and wasn't it exciting! Ah to relive the glorious moments and experience once again, the literal 'smell of the greasepaint and the roar of the crowd'.

These were the good old, bad old days of Sheffield's theatrical history, the like of which we shall never see again. As we stand on the threshold of the millennium, having glimpsed into the past, we must now look forward to the future, not just of the theatre but as they said in the Musical Hall days for 'Chiefly yourselves'!

ABOUT THE AUTHOR

Bryen D Hillerby has lived in the city of Sheffield for over fifteen years and describes it as his 'spiritual home'. 'Married' to the theatre, he has a consuming passion for the arts, coming from a theatrical family background. '*The Lost Theatres of Sheffield*', is his second book, his first being '*The Hippodrome Theatre, Mexborough*', which it is hoped will be revised and reprinted in the near future.

Bryen D Hillerby. 24 February 1999.

Courtesy of Sheffield Newspapers Ltd

Acknowledgements

Mr Douglas Hindmarch and staff of the Local Studies Centre, Sheffield City Library and Information Services for their research assistance. Also for their kind permission to reproduce many of the photographs featured here. Rotherham Metropolitan Borough Council, Library and Information Services, Archives and Local Studies Department, for their kind permission to reproduce the theatres location map.

'*Star*' newspapers, for the provision of *Empire* stage fire, Pavlova and author's photograph.

Also Mr John Highcliffe. Mr Peter Harvey '*The Telegraph*'.

Mr R L Roper, of Bournemouth, without whose years of archive work and generosity with information, this book could not have been written. A lifelong friend, I am indebted and deeply grateful to him for his assistance and support.

Mrs Wendy Valentine for the photograph of her with Dickie Valentine.

Mrs Edna Eyre for the photograph of Laurel and Hardy and Mr Bocking.

Mrs Iris Gibson for the Pavlova flowers and programme.

Mrs Pat Crowther for her photograph of herself as a child.

Mrs Dorothy Butterley for her '*Dracula*', information.

Mrs Sadie Macnamara for *Britannia Theatre* information and the use of photograph of her act.

Mr Danny La Rue who so kindly agreed to write the foreword.

Mrs K Lawton for consultation and word processing services.

Mr Mike Parsons of Pen and Sword Publications.

Mr and Mrs Glen Sanderson for '1940', photograph shoot.

Jane for use of photograph.

Staff of Yorkshire Television for features.

Mr Tony Capstick of BBC Radio Sheffield for interviews.

Mr Peter Johnson, PMC Communications Ltd. for his kind permission to quote extracts from his *Lyceum Theatre* book.

E Lawrence for interior renovation *Lyceum* photograph.

Mr John S O'Neill for the '*Jack and Jill*' programme.

My parents Ralph and Joan Hillerby, for their support and encouragement.

Mrs Nita White, '*South Yorkshire Opera*'.

Mr Malcolm D Broomfield for London accommodation.

Mrs Gill Nelson - the 'Starstore' Sheffield.

Mrs Shirley Harris and Mrs Pam Harcourt for 'Tillers' photographs.

Finally, to all those people that I didn't know but have kindly written to me recallling their fascinating memories of many Sheffield Theatres.